HOME
RENOVATION
PLANNER
& ROOM ORGANISER

Copyright jaymcdesignbooks 2020

FIND, FOLLOW AND LIKE US ON FACEBOOK!
Comments, question and reviews welcome

A BIG THANK YOU FOR SUPPORTING INDEPENDANT PUBLISHING
WE HOPE YOU ARE HAPPY WITH YOUR PURCHASE

REVIEWS ARE IMPORTANT!

Your feedback and comments are greatly appreciated
on Facebook and Amazon. Both help us bring the best to you
and our customers. A few seconds of your valuable time would mean
a huge difference to helping us maintain quality standards
Thank you!

For a great selection of practical and entertaining publications such as
hobby journals, logbooks, planners and diaries as well as colouring,
puzzle and activity books for all ages see our complete catalogue.

Why not Subscribe to our monthly Newsletter?

We promise it to be spam free
and contain only informative
news and updates on all our
latest releases and Editor
monthly recommendations.

SIMPLY SCAN
THE QR CODE

WELCOME TO YOUR
RENOVATION PLANNER

USE THIS PLANNER TO TRACK YOUR REMODELLING PROJECTS AND IDEAS ROOM BY ROOM AND KEEP ALL YOUR INFORMATION IN ONE PLACE

EACH SECTION INCLUDES

LISTS FOR ROOM MEASUREMENTS AND REQUIREMENTS

SPACES TO NOTE DOWN ALL YOUR DECOR AND STYLE GOALS AND IDEAS WITH GREAT SKETCH AREAS FOR FLOOR LAYOUT PLANNING AND DESIGNS

AS WELL AS AN ESSENTIAL COLOUR PALETTE FEATURE TO HELP COLOUR COORDINATE YOUR DECORATIING AND FURNITURE CHOICES.

HOME RENOVATION / ROOM PLANNER

ROOM REQUIREMENTS

DECOR & STYLE

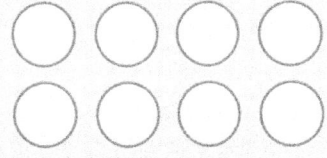

COLOURS

SKETCH PLANS

HOME RENOVATION / PROGRESS TRACKER

WEEKLY GOALS

QUESTIONS & ISSUES

TO-DO'S

MATERIALS LIST

HOME RENOVATION / ROOM PLANNING GRIDS

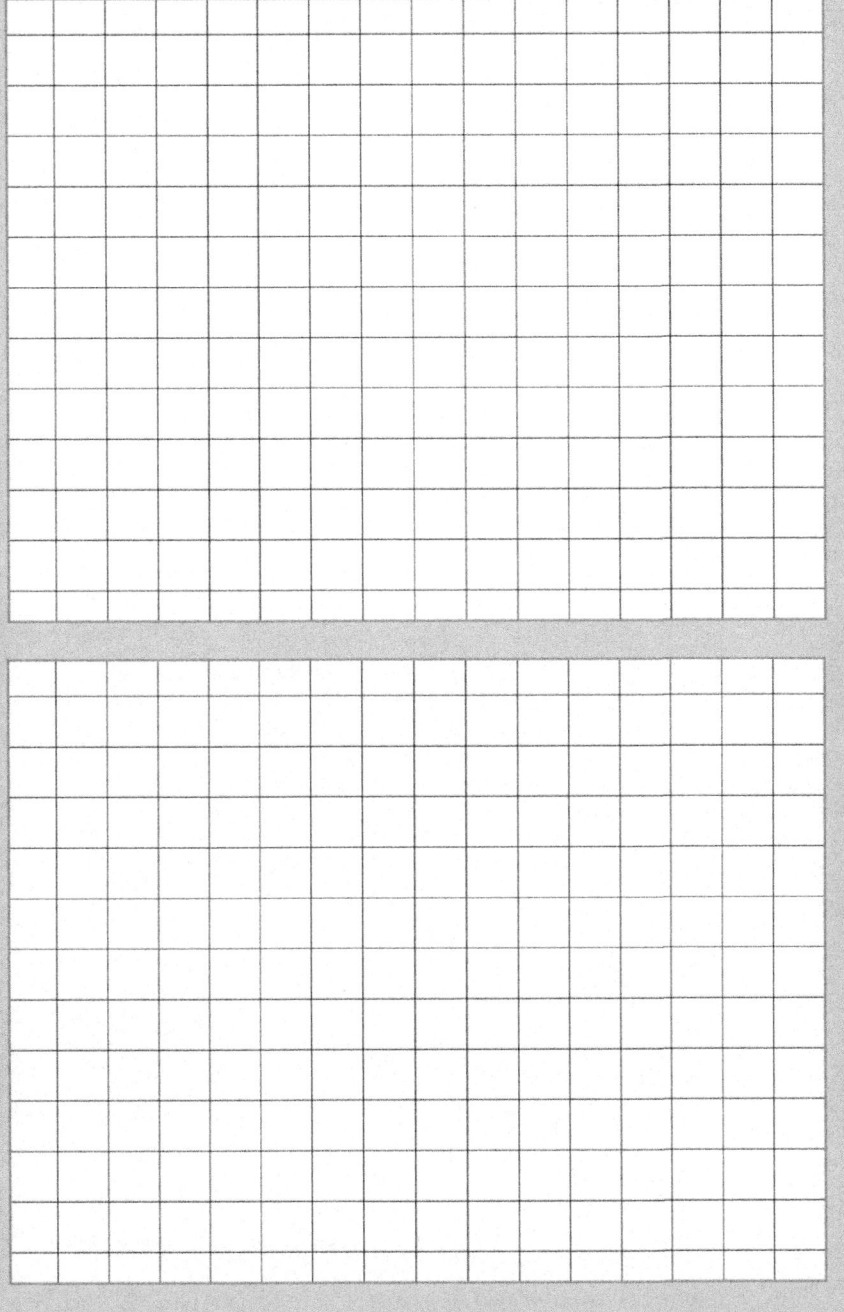

HOME RENOVATION / ROOM PLANNER

ROOM REQUIREMENTS

DECOR & STYLE

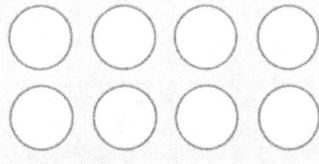

COLOURS

SKETCH PLANS

HOME RENOVATION / PROGRESS TRACKER

WEEKLY GOALS

QUESTIONS & ISSUES

TO-DO'S

MATERIALS LIST

HOME RENOVATION / PROGRESS TRACKER

WEEKLY GOALS

QUESTIONS & ISSUES

TO-DO'S

MATERIALS LIST

HOME RENOVATION / ROOM PLANNING GRIDS

HOME RENOVATION / ROOM PLANNING GRIDS

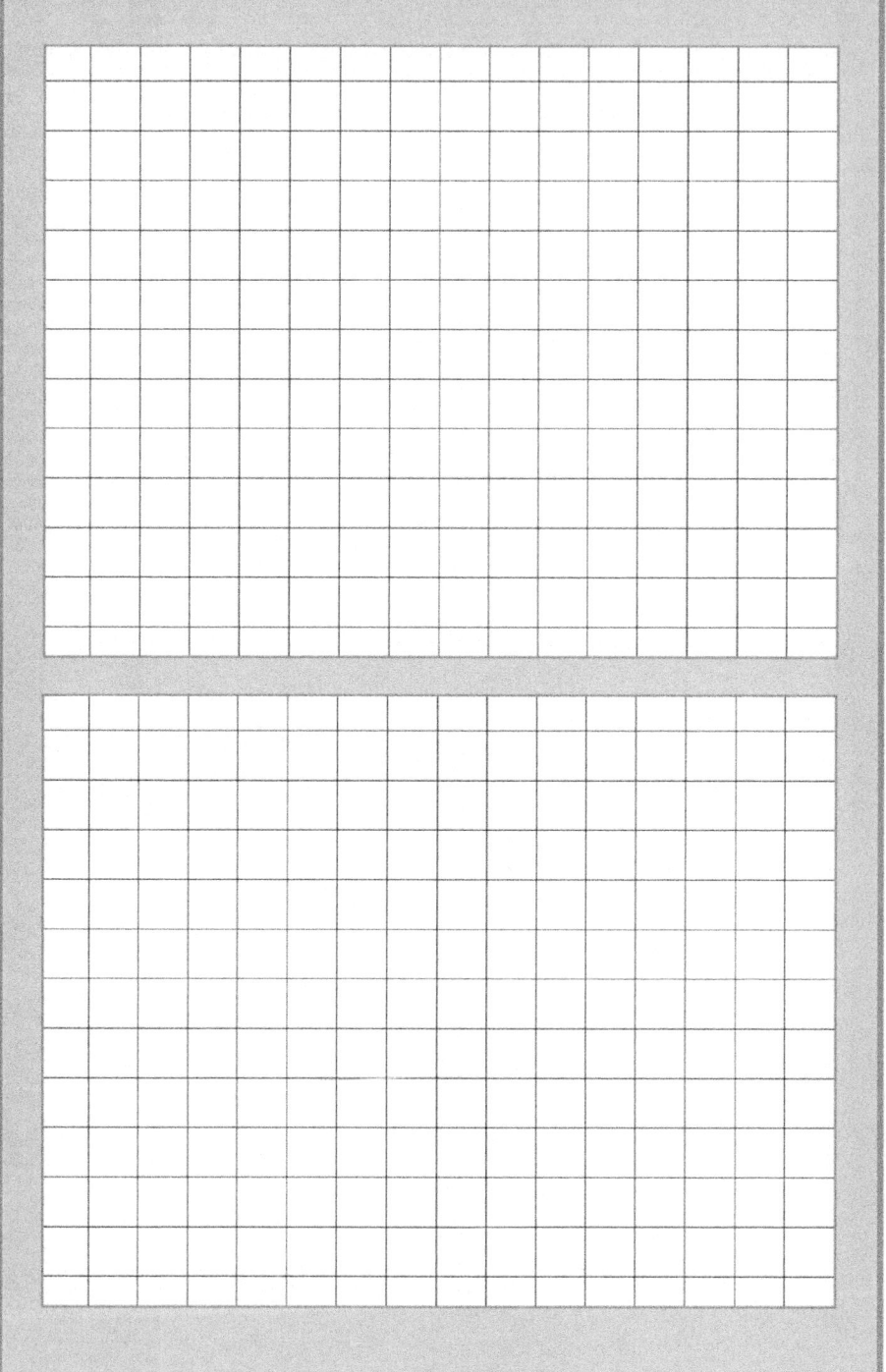

HOME RENOVATION / ROOM PLANNER

ROOM REQUIREMENTS

DECOR & STYLE

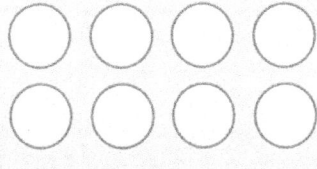

COLOURS

SKETCH PLANS

HOME RENOVATION / PROGRESS TRACKER

WEEKLY GOALS

QUESTIONS & ISSUES

TO-DO'S

MATERIALS LIST

HOME RENOVATION / ROOM PLANNING GRIDS

HOME RENOVATION / ROOM PLANNER

ROOM REQUIREMENTS

DECOR & STYLE

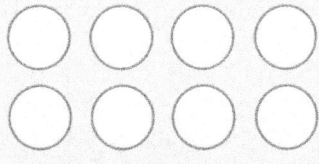

COLOURS

SKETCH PLANS

HOME RENOVATION / PROGRESS TRACKER

WEEKLY GOALS

QUESTIONS & ISSUES

TO-DO'S

MATERIALS LIST

HOME RENOVATION / PROGRESS TRACKER

WEEKLY GOALS

QUESTIONS & ISSUES

TO-DO'S

MATERIALS LIST

HOME RENOVATION / ROOM PLANNING GRIDS

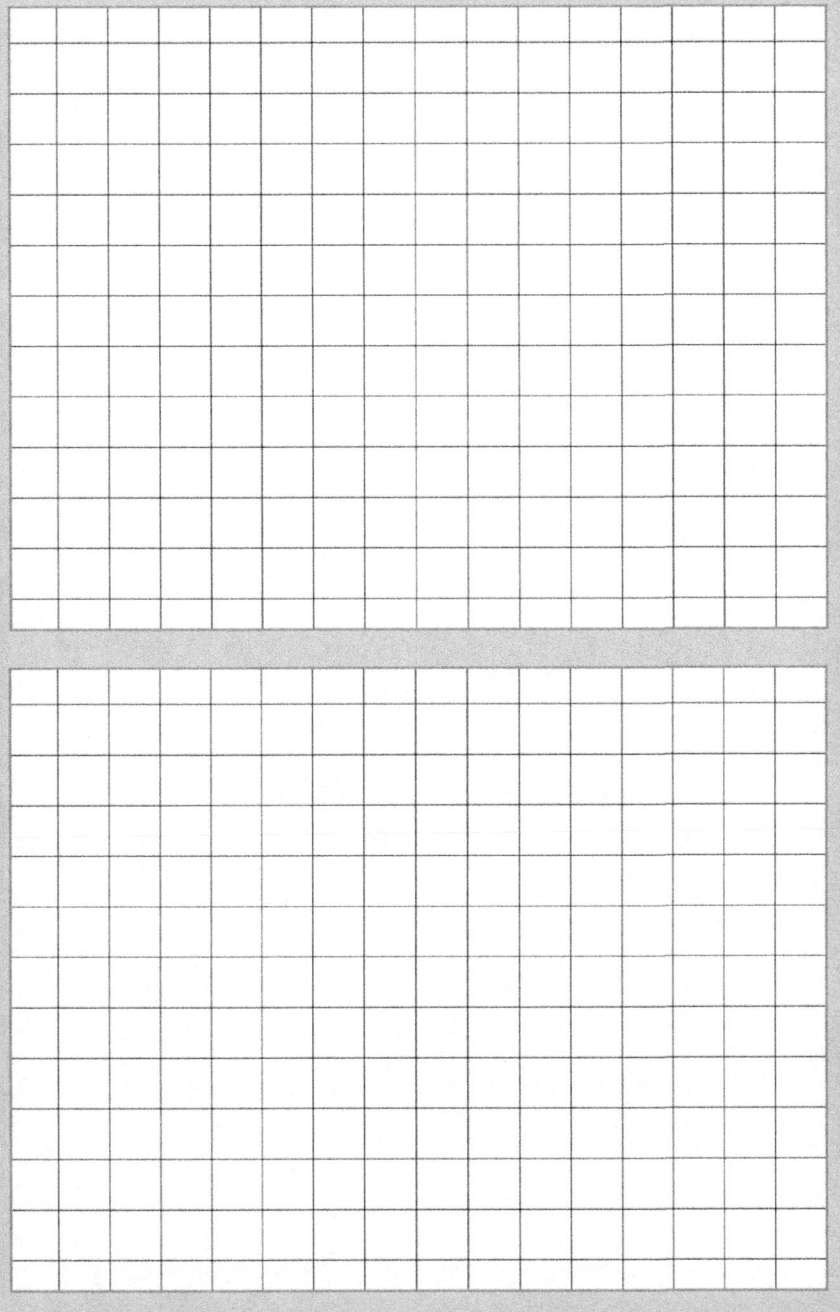

HOME RENOVATION / ROOM PLANNER

ROOM REQUIREMENTS

DECOR & STYLE

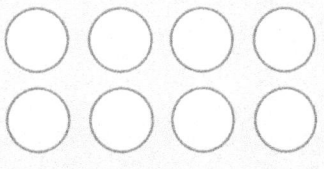

COLOURS

SKETCH PLANS

HOME RENOVATION / PROGRESS TRACKER

WEEKLY GOALS

QUESTIONS & ISSUES

TO-DO'S

MATERIALS LIST

HOME RENOVATION / ROOM PLANNING GRIDS

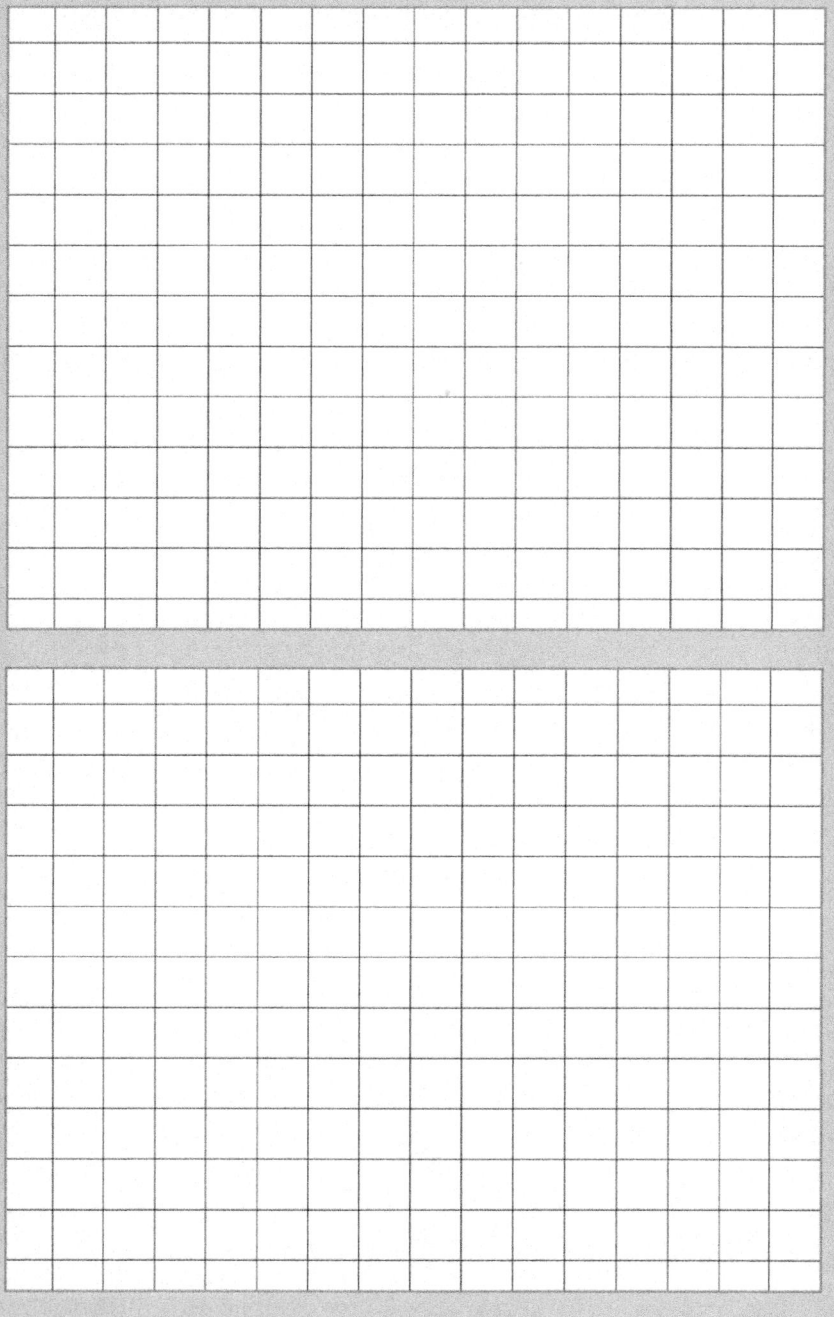

HOME RENOVATION / ROOM PLANNER

ROOM REQUIREMENTS

DECOR & STYLE

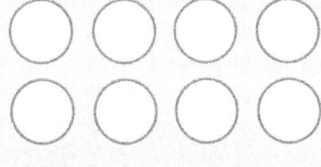

COLOURS

SKETCH PLANS

HOME RENOVATION / PROGRESS TRACKER

WEEKLY GOALS

QUESTIONS & ISSUES

TO-DO'S

MATERIALS LIST

HOME RENOVATION / ROOM PLANNING GRIDS

HOME RENOVATION / ROOM PLANNER

ROOM REQUIREMENTS

DECOR & STYLE

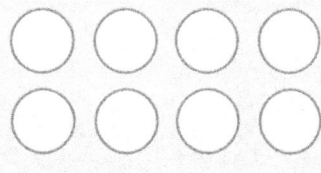

COLOURS

SKETCH PLANS

HOME RENOVATION / PROGRESS TRACKER

WEEKLY GOALS

QUESTIONS & ISSUES

TO-DO'S

MATERIALS LIST

HOME RENOVATION / ROOM PLANNING GRIDS

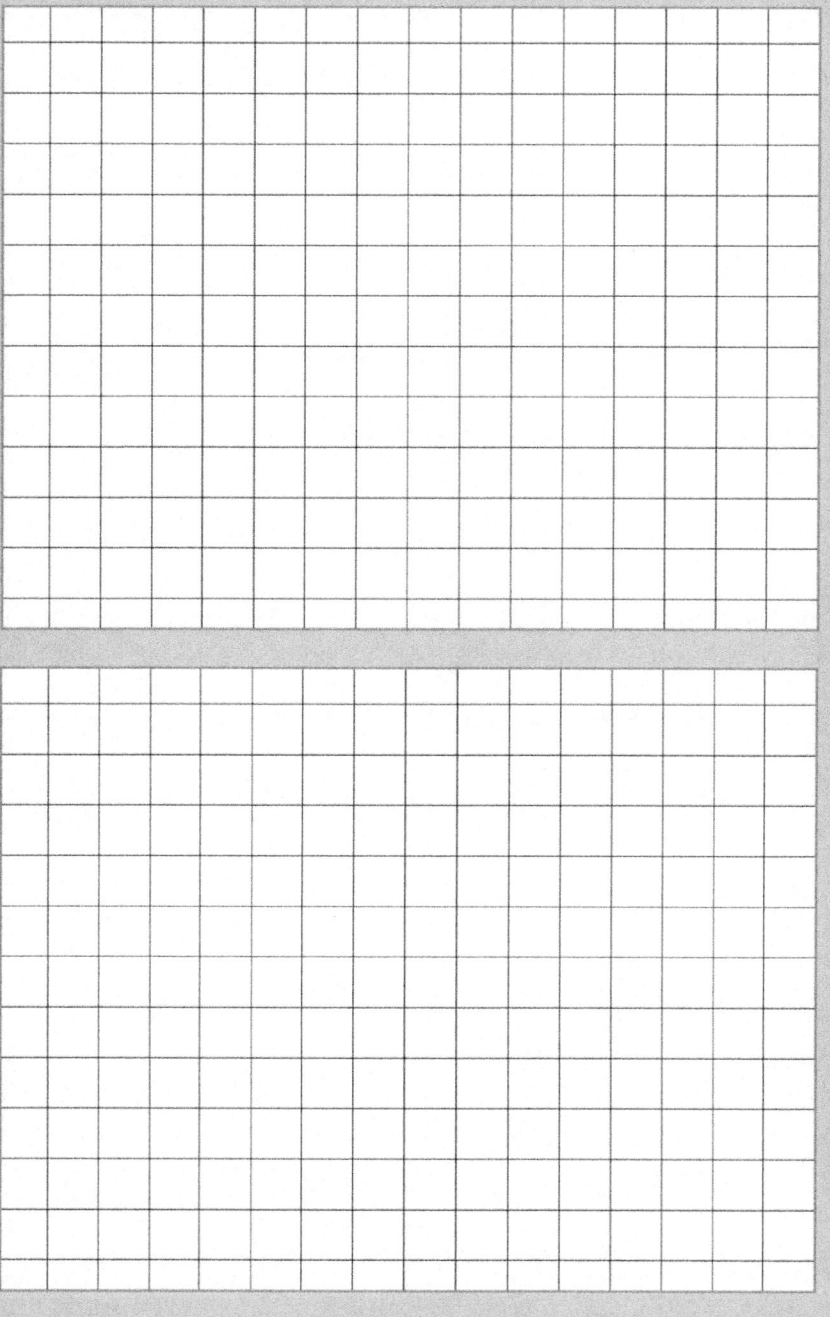

HOME RENOVATION / ROOM PLANNER

ROOM REQUIREMENTS

DECOR & STYLE

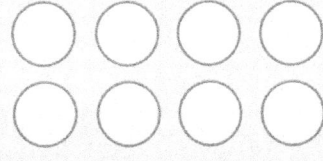

COLOURS

SKETCH PLANS

HOME RENOVATION / PROGRESS TRACKER

WEEKLY GOALS

QUESTIONS & ISSUES

TO-DO'S

MATERIALS LIST

HOME RENOVATION / ROOM PLANNING GRIDS

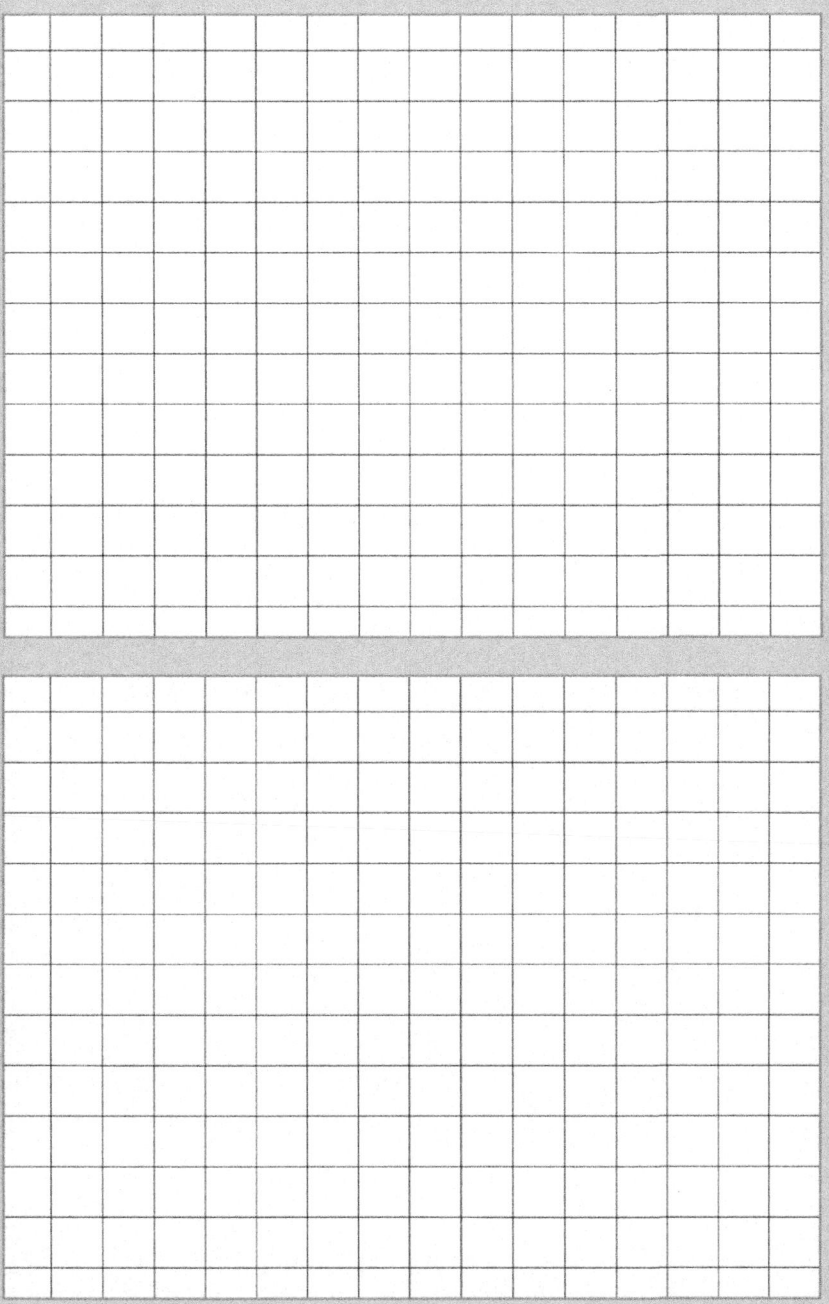

HOME RENOVATION / ROOM PLANNER

ROOM REQUIREMENTS

DECOR & STYLE

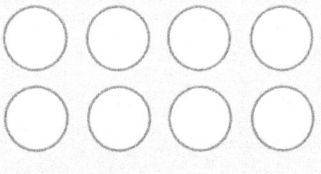

COLOURS

SKETCH PLANS

HOME RENOVATION / PROGRESS TRACKER

WEEKLY GOALS

QUESTIONS & ISSUES

TO-DO'S

MATERIALS LIST

HOME RENOVATION / ROOM PLANNING GRIDS

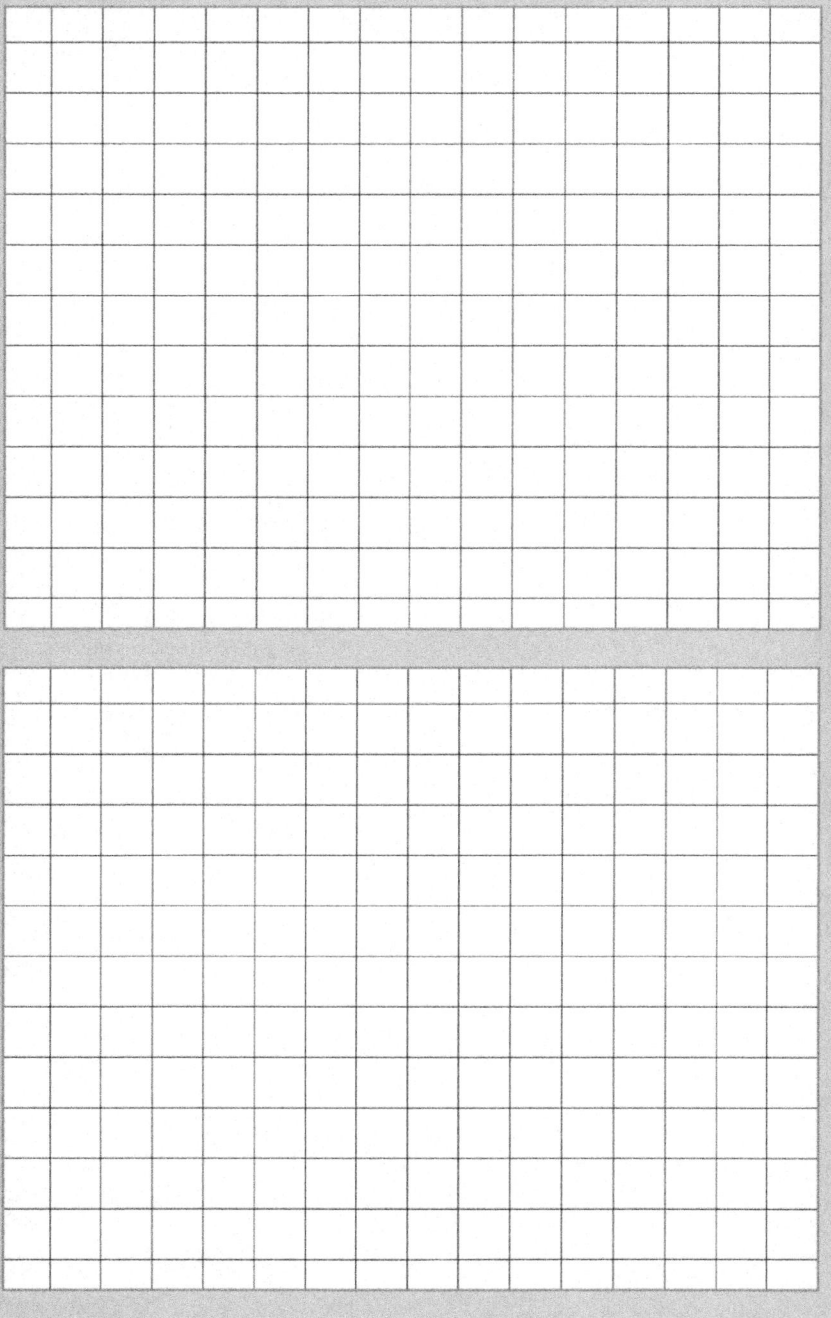

HOME RENOVATION / ROOM PLANNER

ROOM REQUIREMENTS

DECOR & STYLE

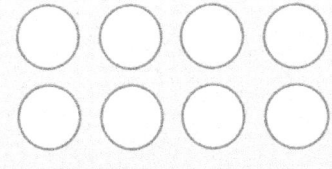

COLOURS

SKETCH PLANS

HOME RENOVATION / PROGRESS TRACKER

WEEKLY GOALS

QUESTIONS & ISSUES

TO-DO'S

MATERIALS LIST

HOME RENOVATION / ROOM PLANNING GRIDS

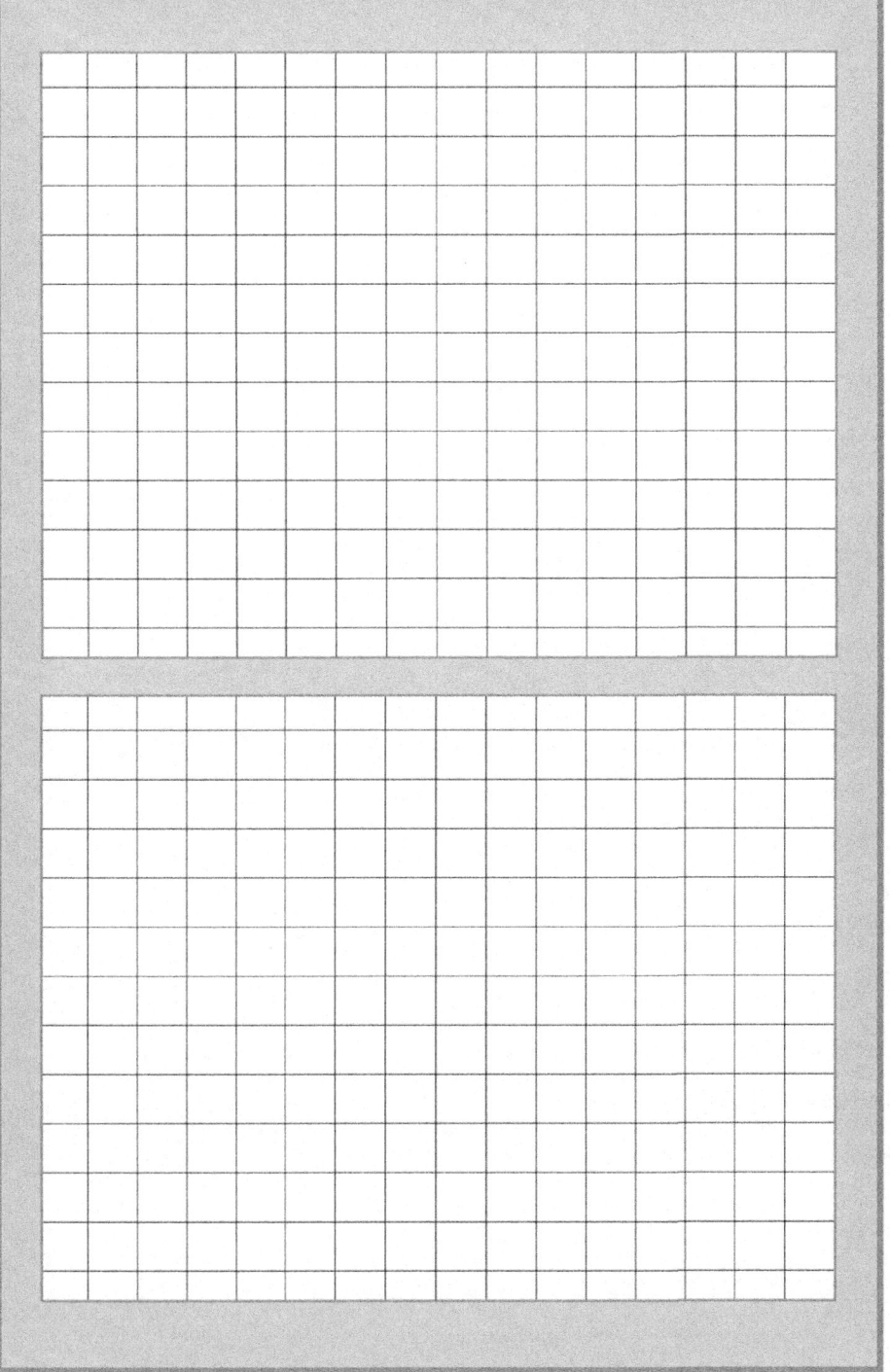

HOME RENOVATION / ROOM PLANNER

ROOM REQUIREMENTS

DECOR & STYLE

COLOURS

SKETCH PLANS

HOME RENOVATION / PROGRESS TRACKER

WEEKLY GOALS

QUESTIONS & ISSUES

TO-DO'S

MATERIALS LIST

HOME RENOVATION / ROOM PLANNING GRIDS

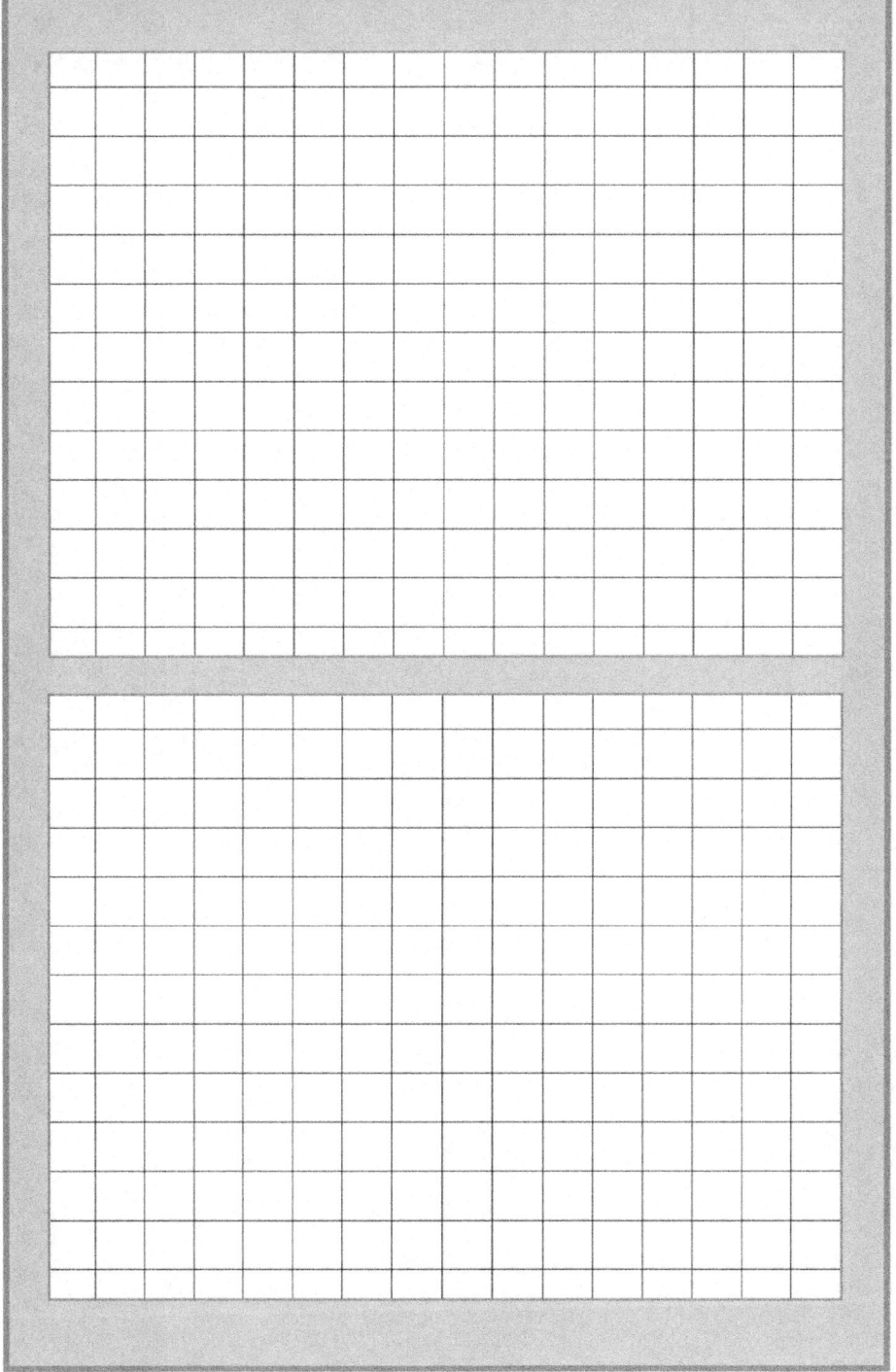

HOME RENOVATION / ROOM PLANNER

ROOM REQUIREMENTS

DECOR & STYLE

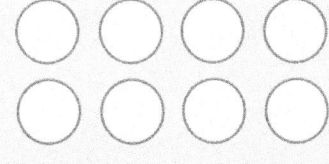

COLOURS

SKETCH PLANS

HOME RENOVATION / PROGRESS TRACKER

WEEKLY GOALS

QUESTIONS & ISSUES

TO-DO'S

MATERIALS LIST

HOME RENOVATION / ROOM PLANNING GRIDS

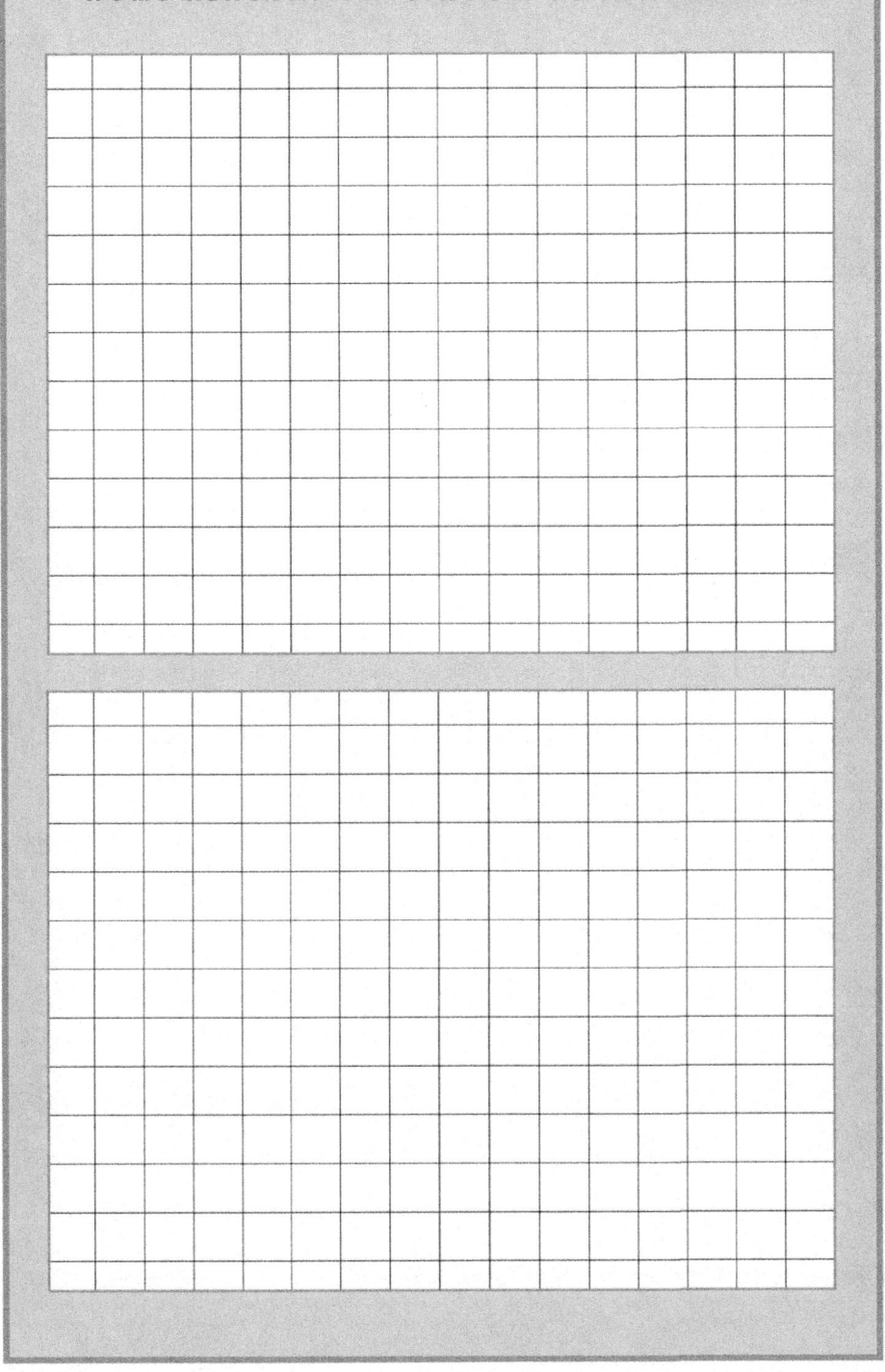

HOME RENOVATION / ROOM PLANNER

ROOM REQUIREMENTS

DECOR & STYLE

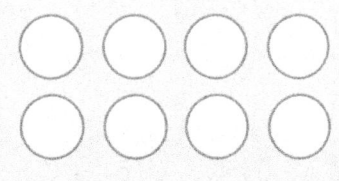

COLOURS

SKETCH PLANS

HOME RENOVATION / PROGRESS TRACKER

WEEKLY GOALS

QUESTIONS & ISSUES

TO-DO'S

MATERIALS LIST

HOME RENOVATION / ROOM PLANNING GRIDS

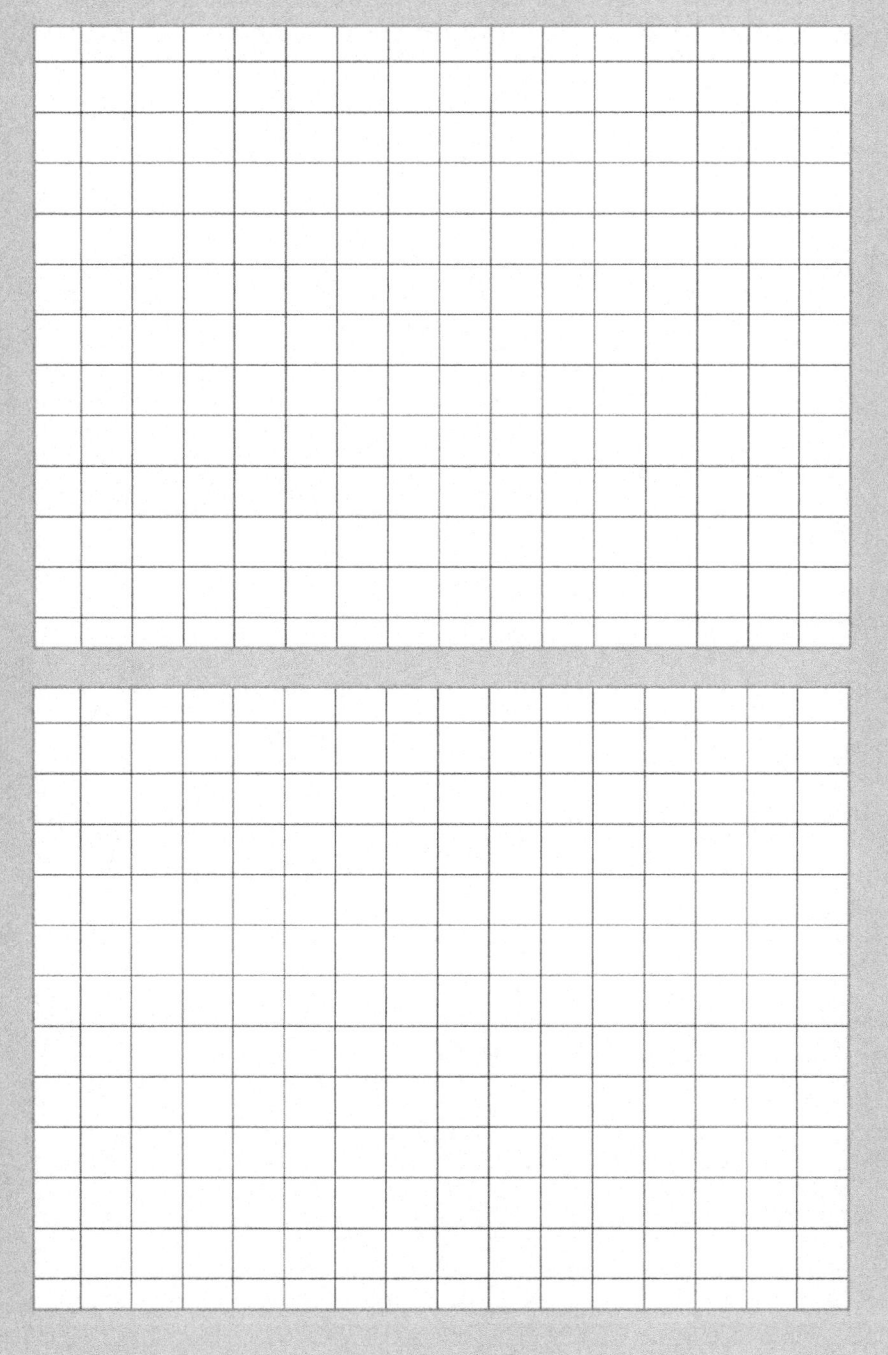

HOME RENOVATION / ROOM PLANNER

ROOM REQUIREMENTS

DECOR & STYLE

COLOURS

SKETCH PLANS

HOME RENOVATION / PROGRESS TRACKER

WEEKLY GOALS

QUESTIONS & ISSUES

TO-DO'S

MATERIALS LIST

HOME RENOVATION / ROOM PLANNING GRIDS

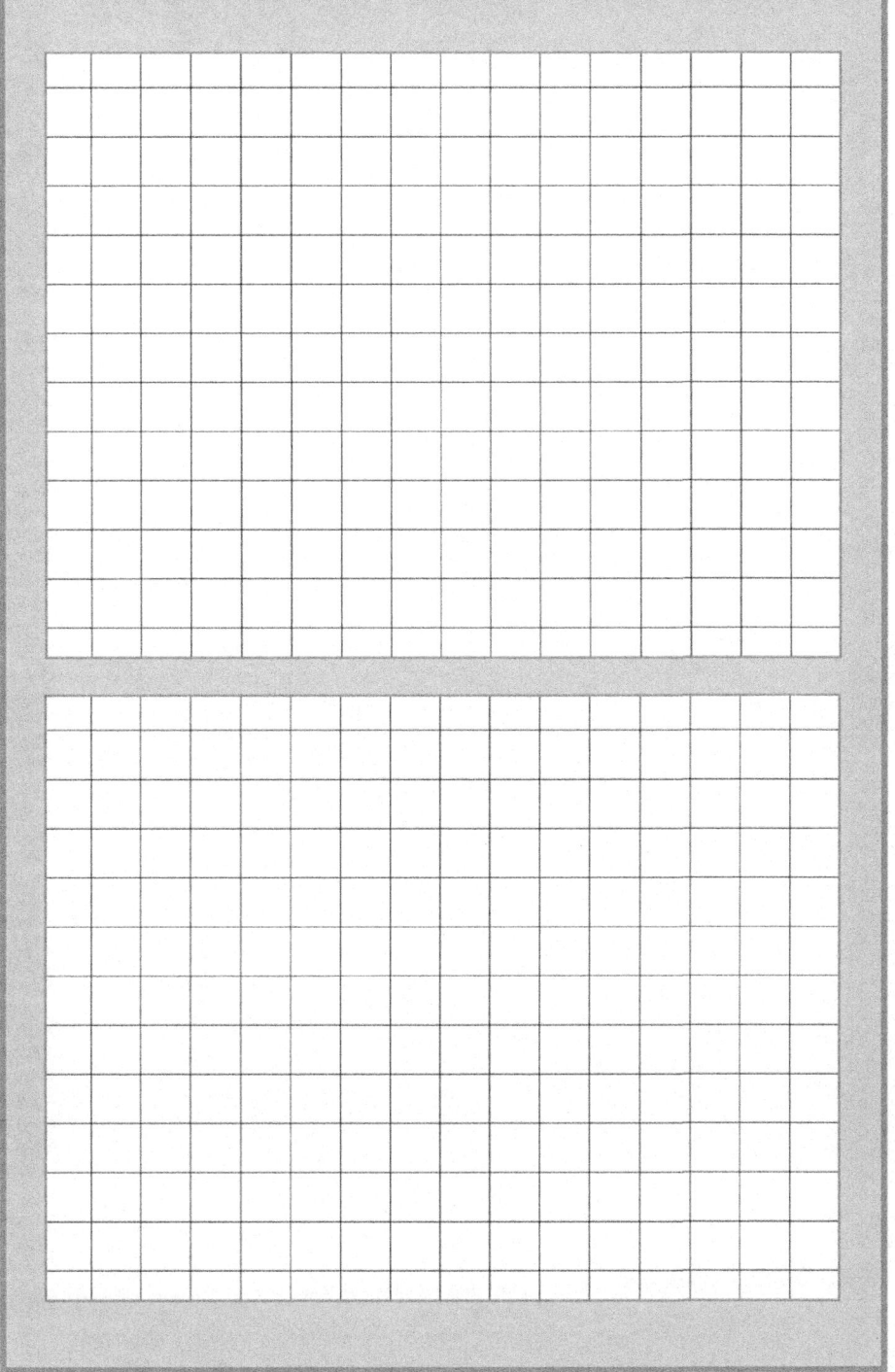

HOME RENOVATION / ROOM PLANNER

ROOM REQUIREMENTS

DECOR & STYLE

COLOURS

SKETCH PLANS

HOME RENOVATION / PROGRESS TRACKER

WEEKLY GOALS

QUESTIONS & ISSUES

TO-DO'S

MATERIALS LIST

HOME RENOVATION / ROOM PLANNING GRIDS

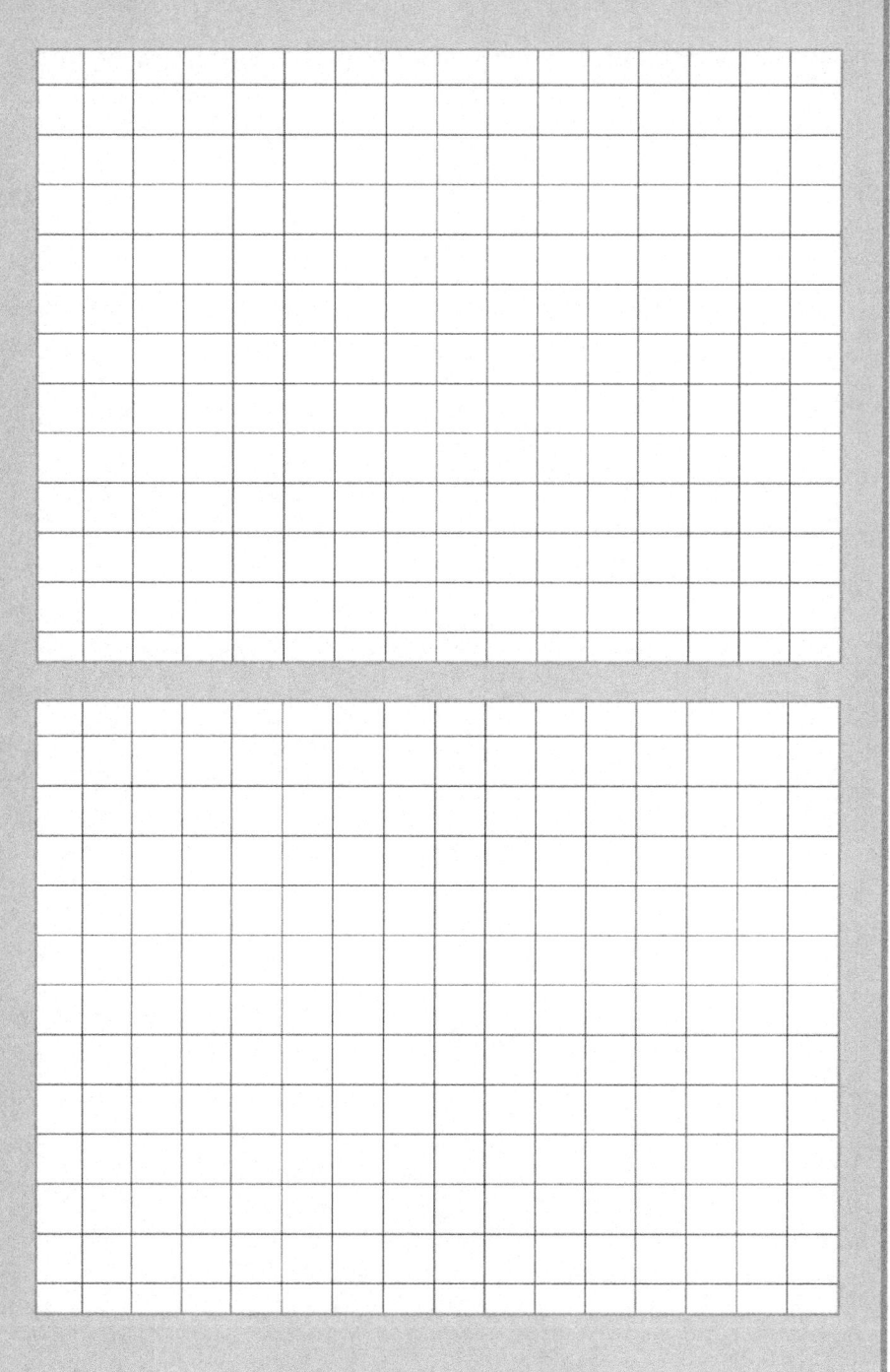

HOME RENOVATION / ROOM PLANNER

ROOM REQUIREMENTS

DECOR & STYLE

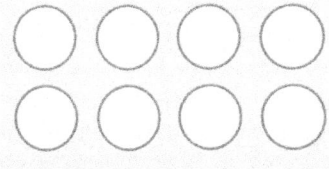

COLOURS

SKETCH PLANS

HOME RENOVATION / PROGRESS TRACKER

WEEKLY GOALS

QUESTIONS & ISSUES

TO-DO'S

MATERIALS LIST

HOME RENOVATION / ROOM PLANNING GRIDS

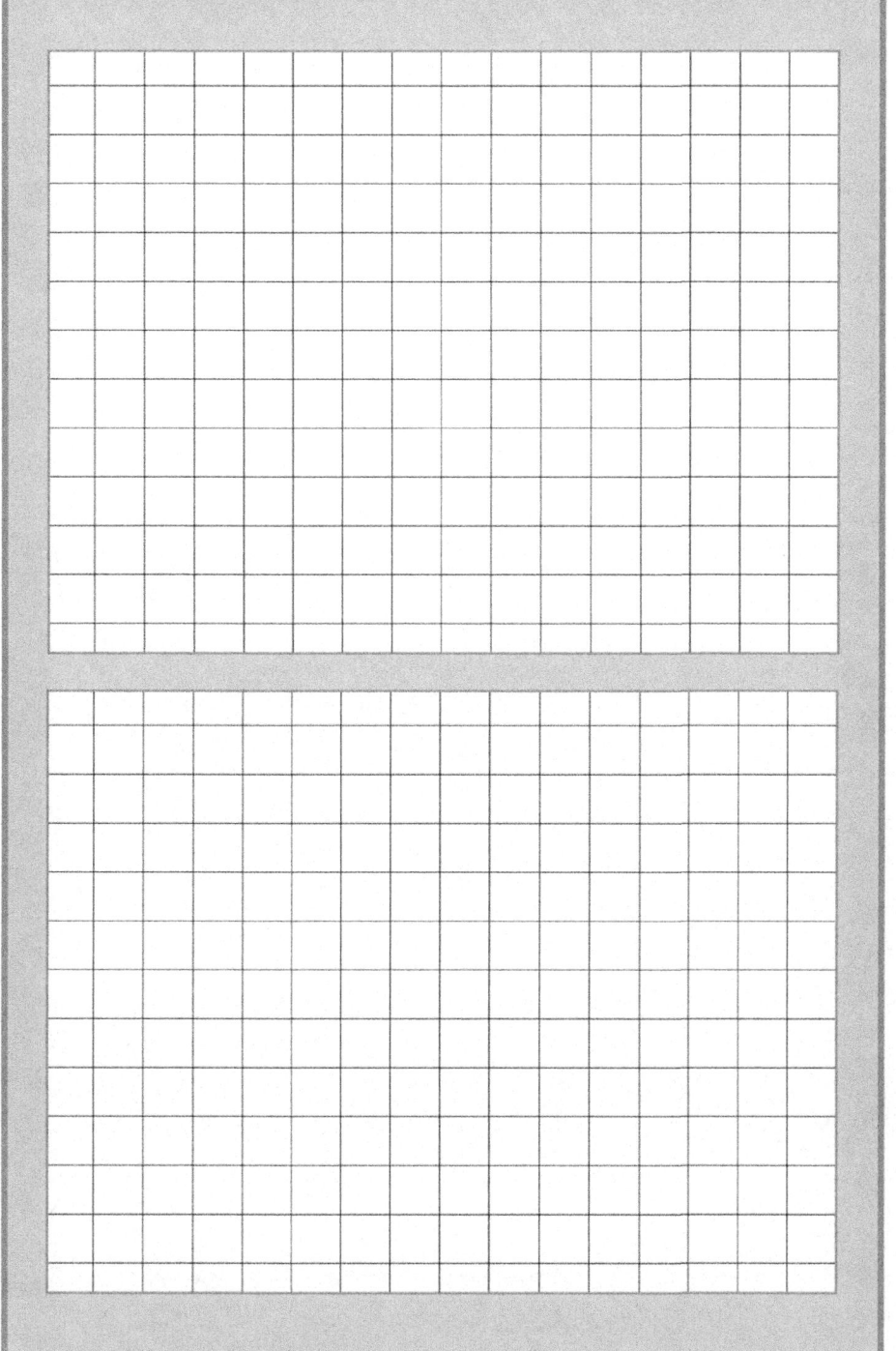

HOME RENOVATION / ROOM PLANNER

ROOM REQUIREMENTS

DECOR & STYLE

COLOURS

SKETCH PLANS

HOME RENOVATION / PROGRESS TRACKER

WEEKLY GOALS

QUESTIONS & ISSUES

TO-DO'S

MATERIALS LIST

HOME RENOVATION / ROOM PLANNING GRIDS

HOME RENOVATION / ROOM PLANNER

ROOM REQUIREMENTS

DECOR & STYLE

COLOURS

SKETCH PLANS

HOME RENOVATION / PROGRESS TRACKER

WEEKLY GOALS

QUESTIONS & ISSUES

TO-DO'S

MATERIALS LIST

HOME RENOVATION / ROOM PLANNING GRIDS

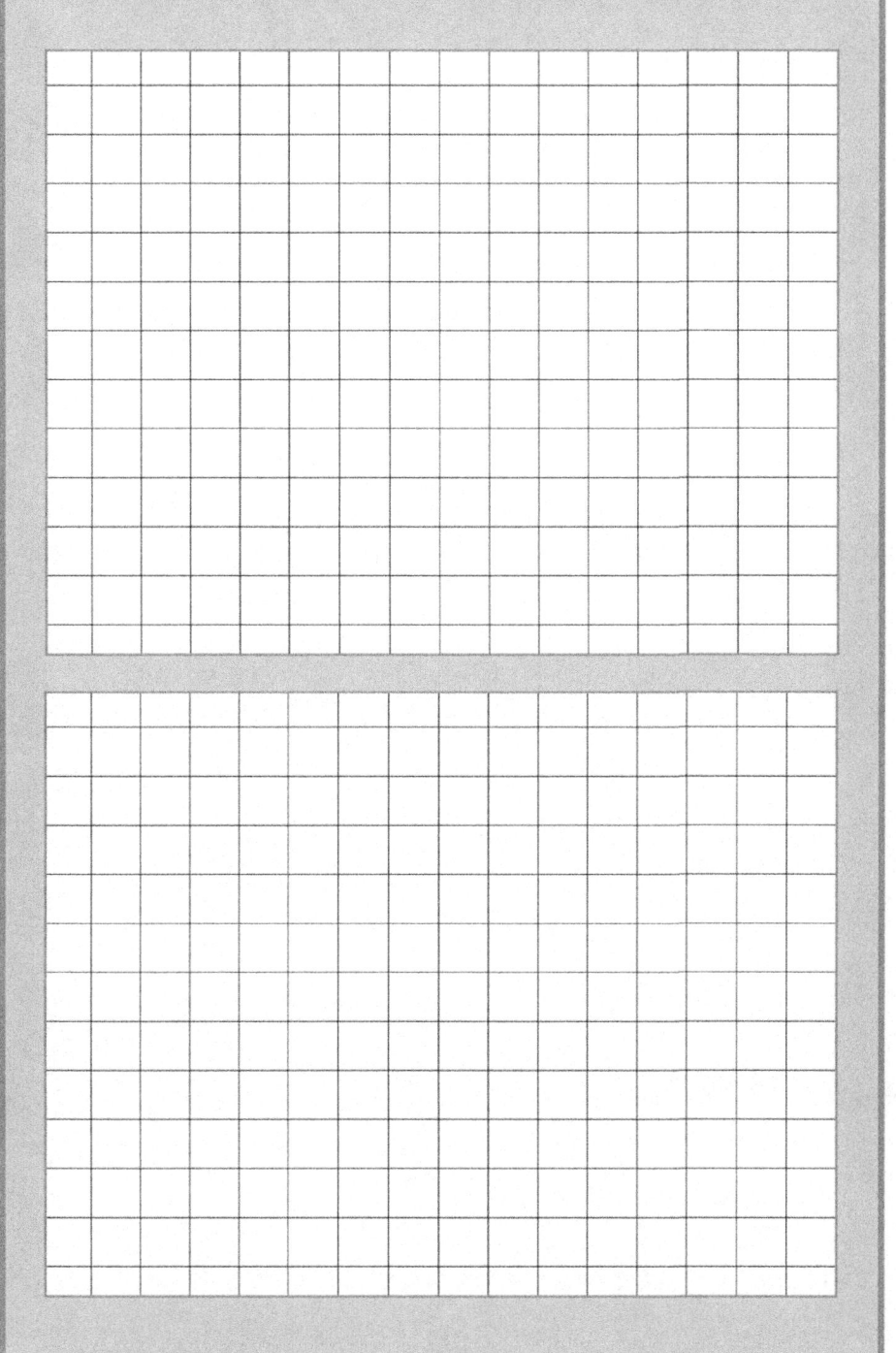

HOME RENOVATION / ROOM PLANNER

ROOM REQUIREMENTS

DECOR & STYLE

COLOURS

SKETCH PLANS

HOME RENOVATION / PROGRESS TRACKER

WEEKLY GOALS

QUESTIONS & ISSUES

TO-DO'S

MATERIALS LIST

HOME RENOVATION / ROOM PLANNING GRIDS

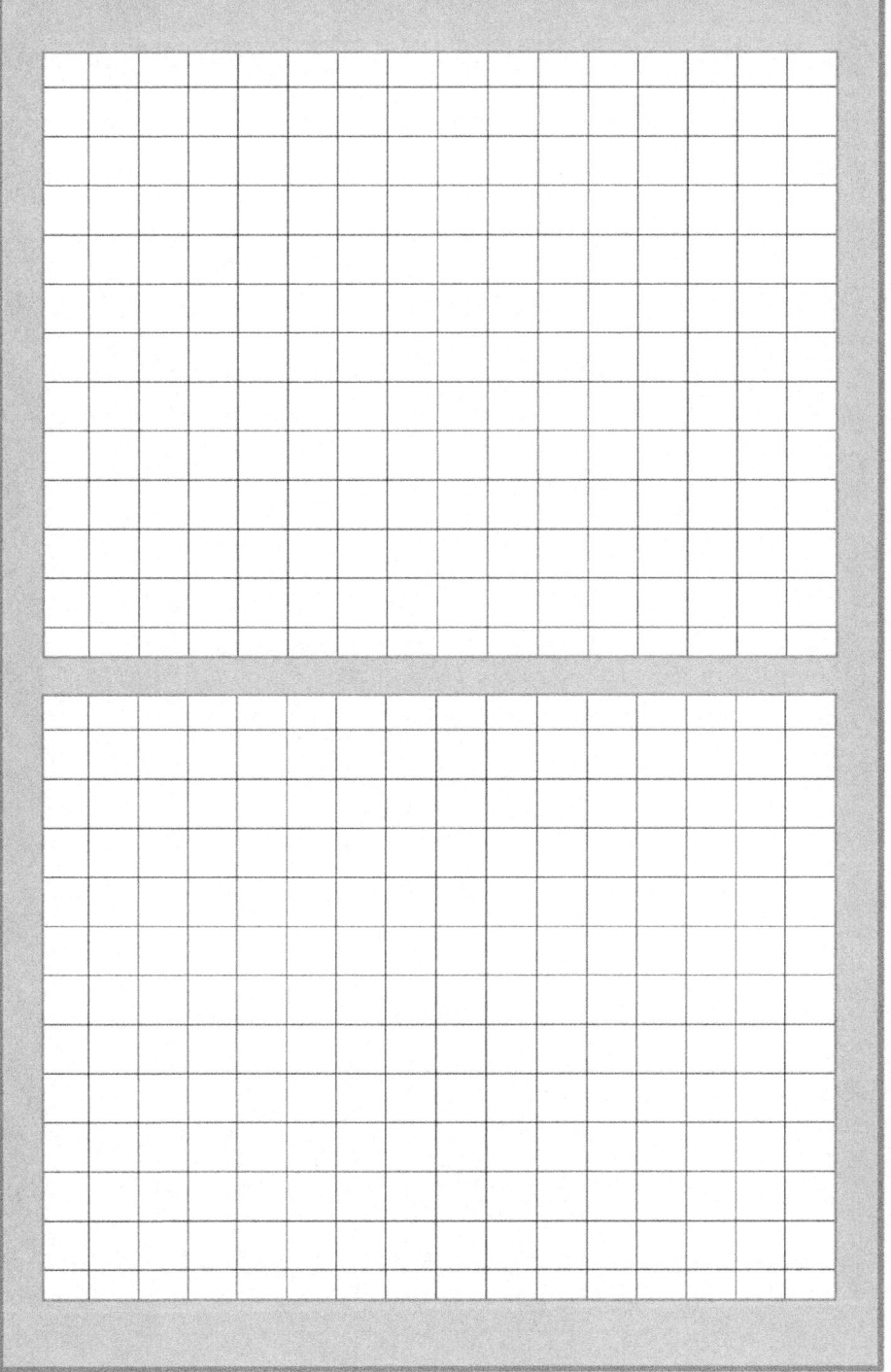

HOME RENOVATION / ROOM PLANNER

ROOM REQUIREMENTS

DECOR & STYLE

COLOURS

SKETCH PLANS

HOME RENOVATION / PROGRESS TRACKER

WEEKLY GOALS

QUESTIONS & ISSUES

TO-DO'S

MATERIALS LIST

HOME RENOVATION / ROOM PLANNING GRIDS

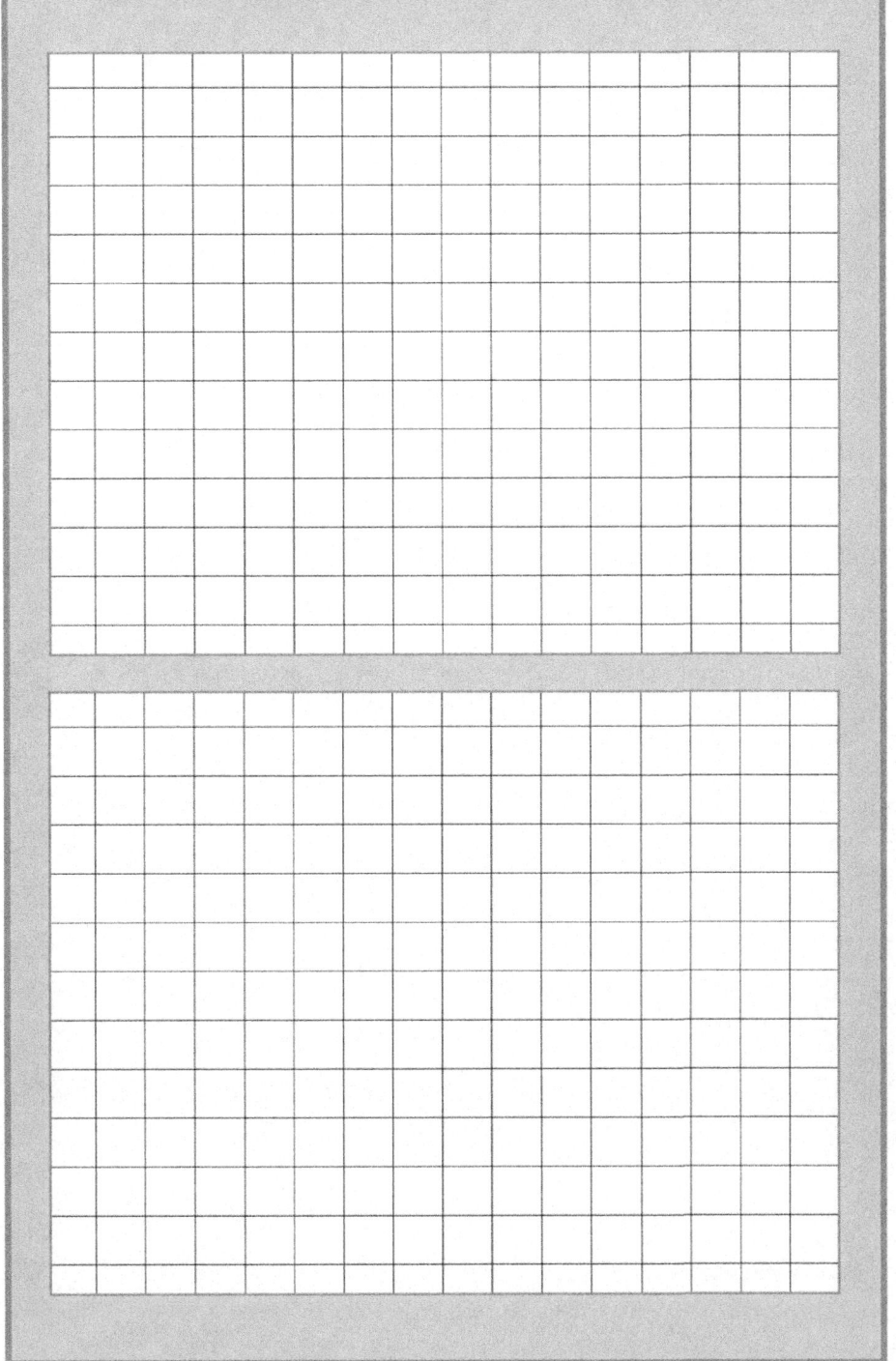

HOME RENOVATION / ROOM PLANNER

ROOM REQUIREMENTS

DECOR & STYLE

COLOURS

SKETCH PLANS

HOME RENOVATION / PROGRESS TRACKER

WEEKLY GOALS

QUESTIONS & ISSUES

TO-DO'S

MATERIALS LIST

HOME RENOVATION / ROOM PLANNING GRIDS

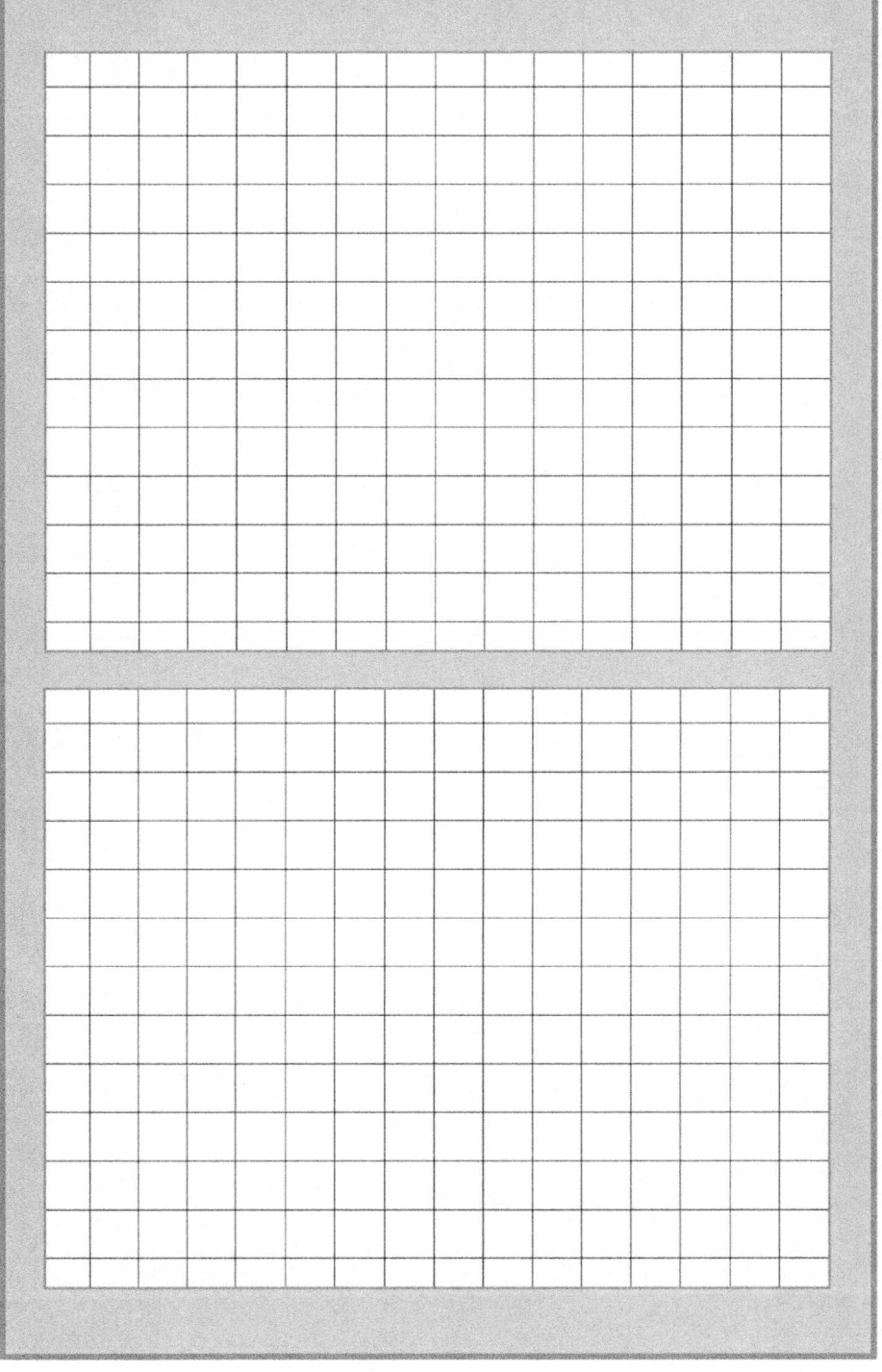

HOME RENOVATION / ROOM PLANNER

ROOM REQUIREMENTS

DECOR & STYLE

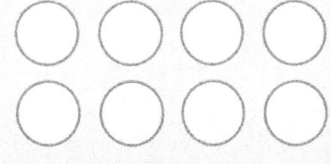

COLOURS

SKETCH PLANS

HOME RENOVATION / PROGRESS TRACKER

WEEKLY GOALS

QUESTIONS & ISSUES

TO-DO'S

MATERIALS LIST

HOME RENOVATION / ROOM PLANNING GRIDS

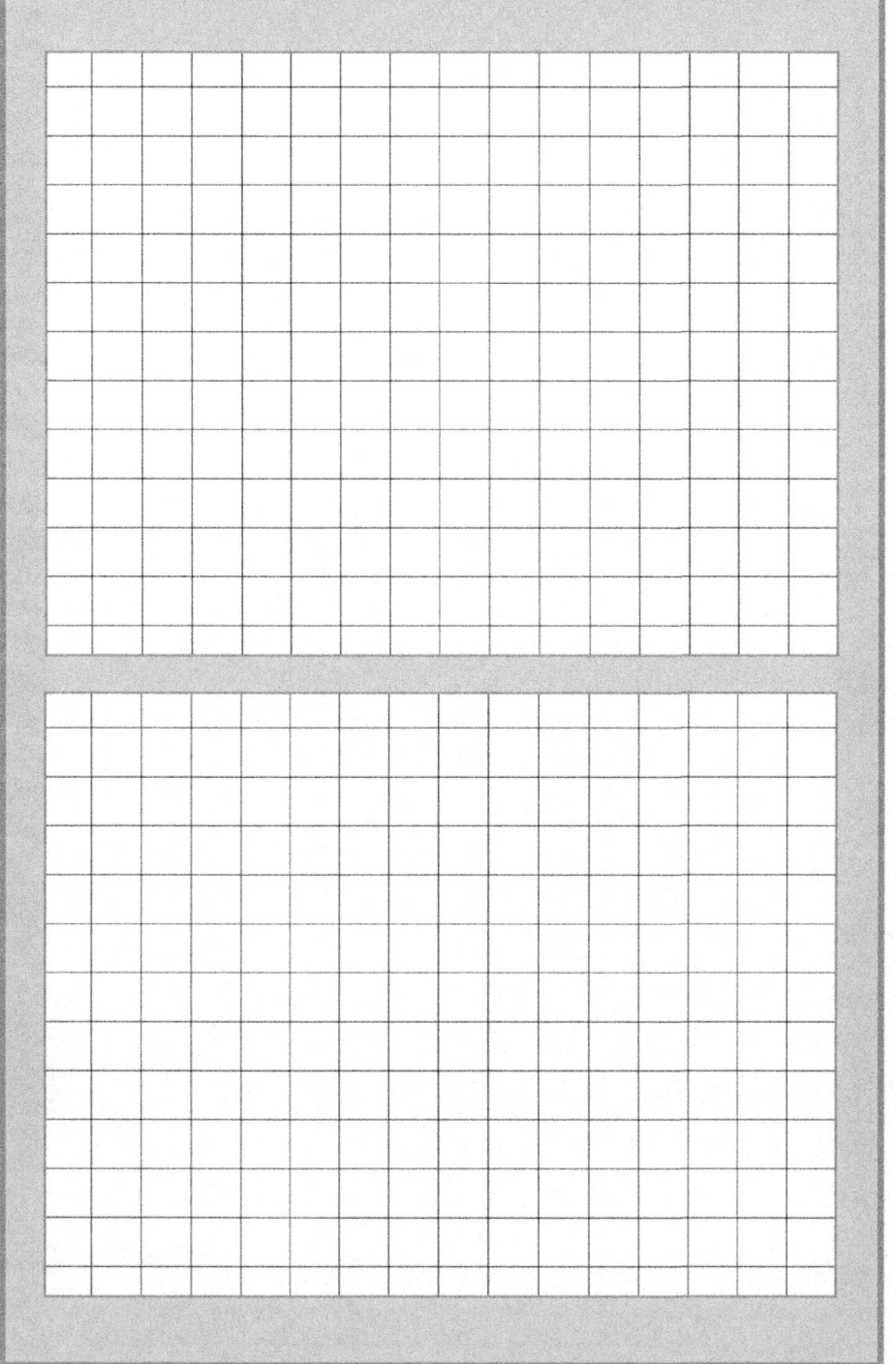

HOME RENOVATION / ROOM PLANNER

ROOM REQUIREMENTS

DECOR & STYLE

COLOURS

SKETCH PLANS

HOME RENOVATION / PROGRESS TRACKER

WEEKLY GOALS

QUESTIONS & ISSUES

TO-DO'S

MATERIALS LIST

HOME RENOVATION / ROOM PLANNING GRIDS

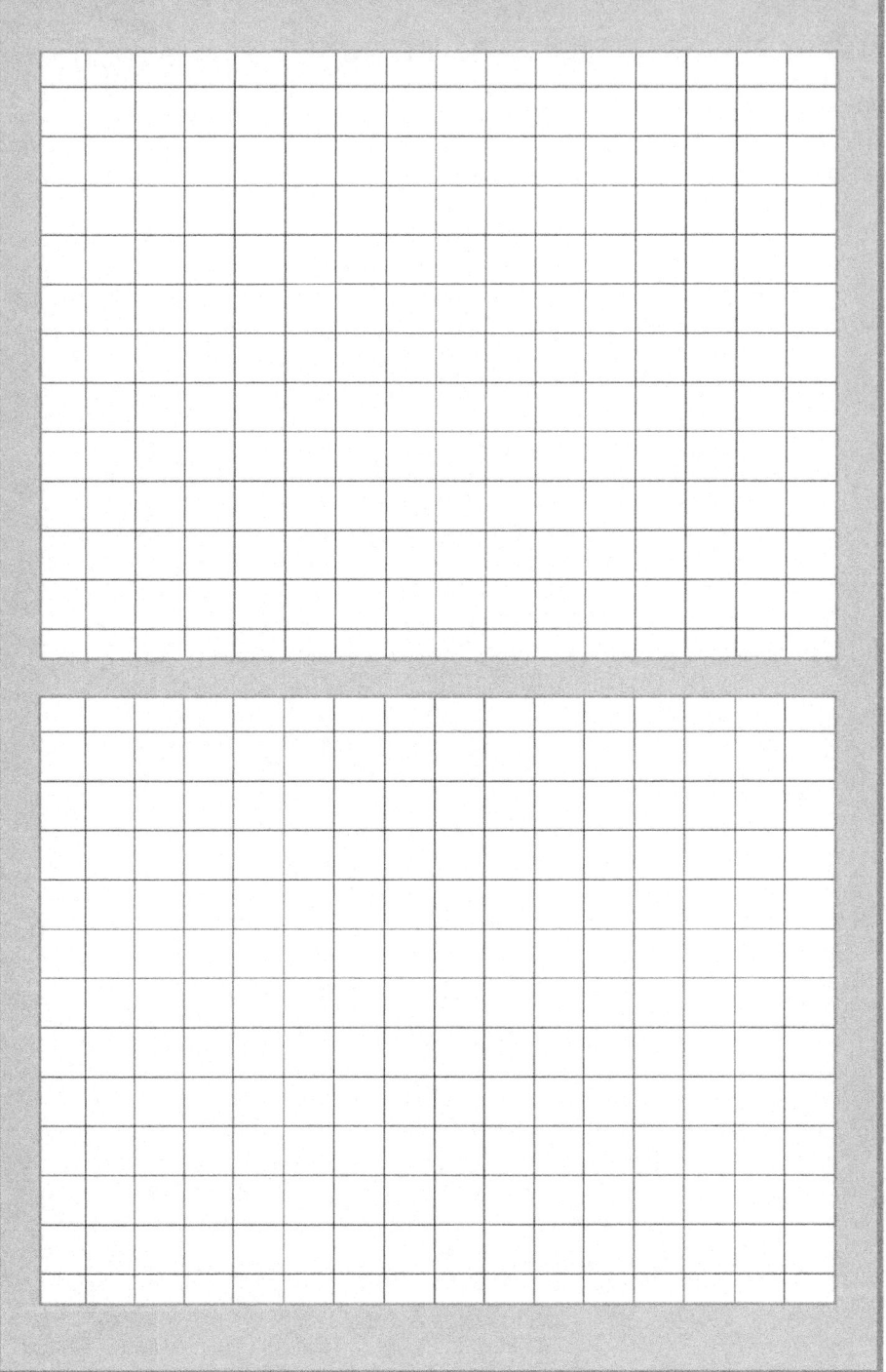

HOME RENOVATION / ROOM PLANNER

ROOM REQUIREMENTS

DECOR & STYLE

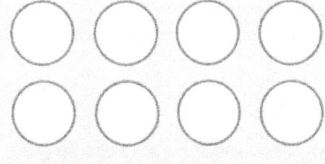

COLOURS

SKETCH PLANS

HOME RENOVATION / PROGRESS TRACKER

WEEKLY GOALS

QUESTIONS & ISSUES

TO-DO'S

MATERIALS LIST

HOME RENOVATION / ROOM PLANNING GRIDS

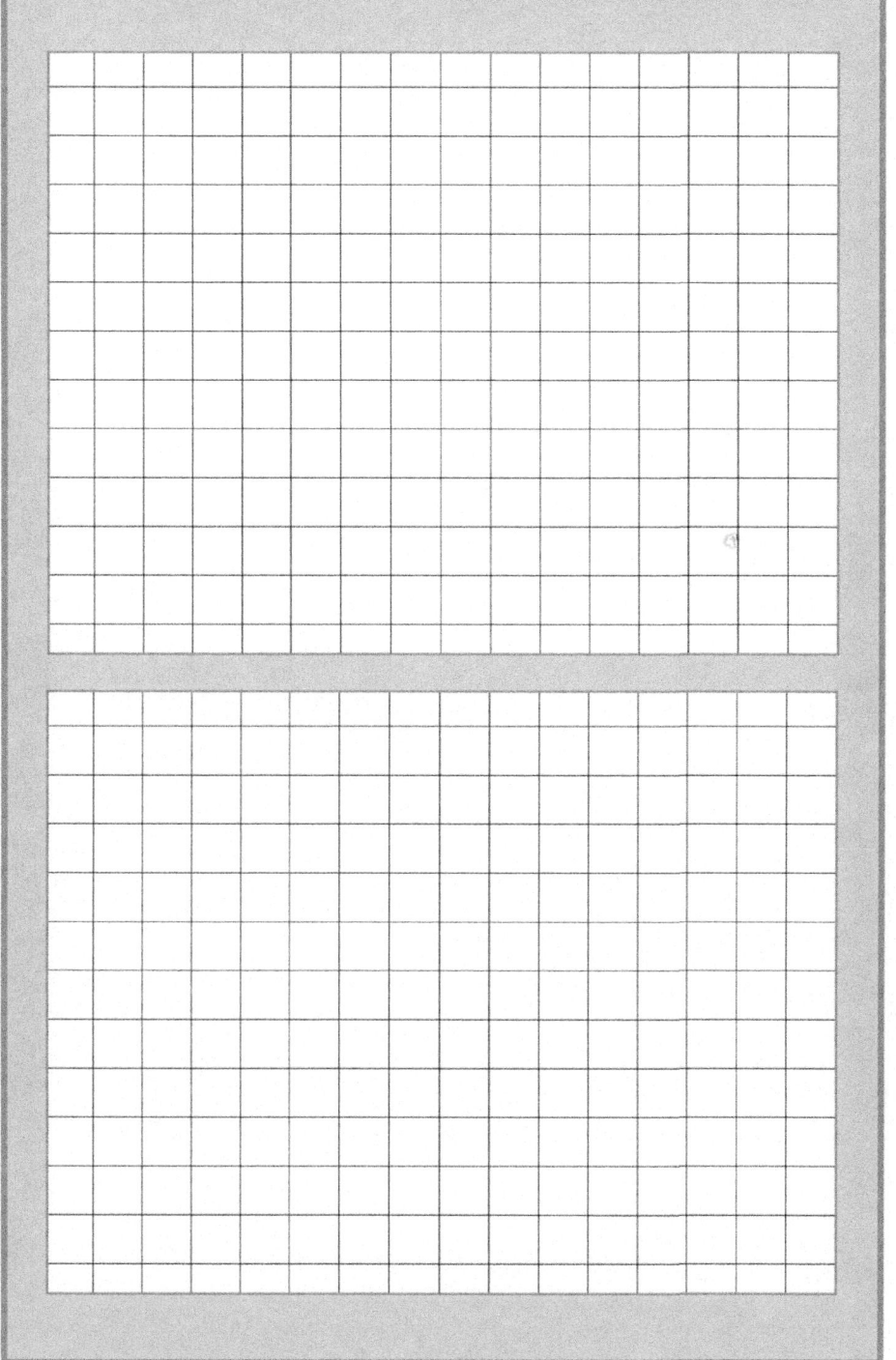

HOME RENOVATION / ROOM PLANNER

ROOM REQUIREMENTS

DECOR & STYLE

COLOURS

SKETCH PLANS

HOME RENOVATION / PROGRESS TRACKER

WEEKLY GOALS

QUESTIONS & ISSUES

TO-DO'S

MATERIALS LIST

HOME RENOVATION / ROOM PLANNING GRIDS

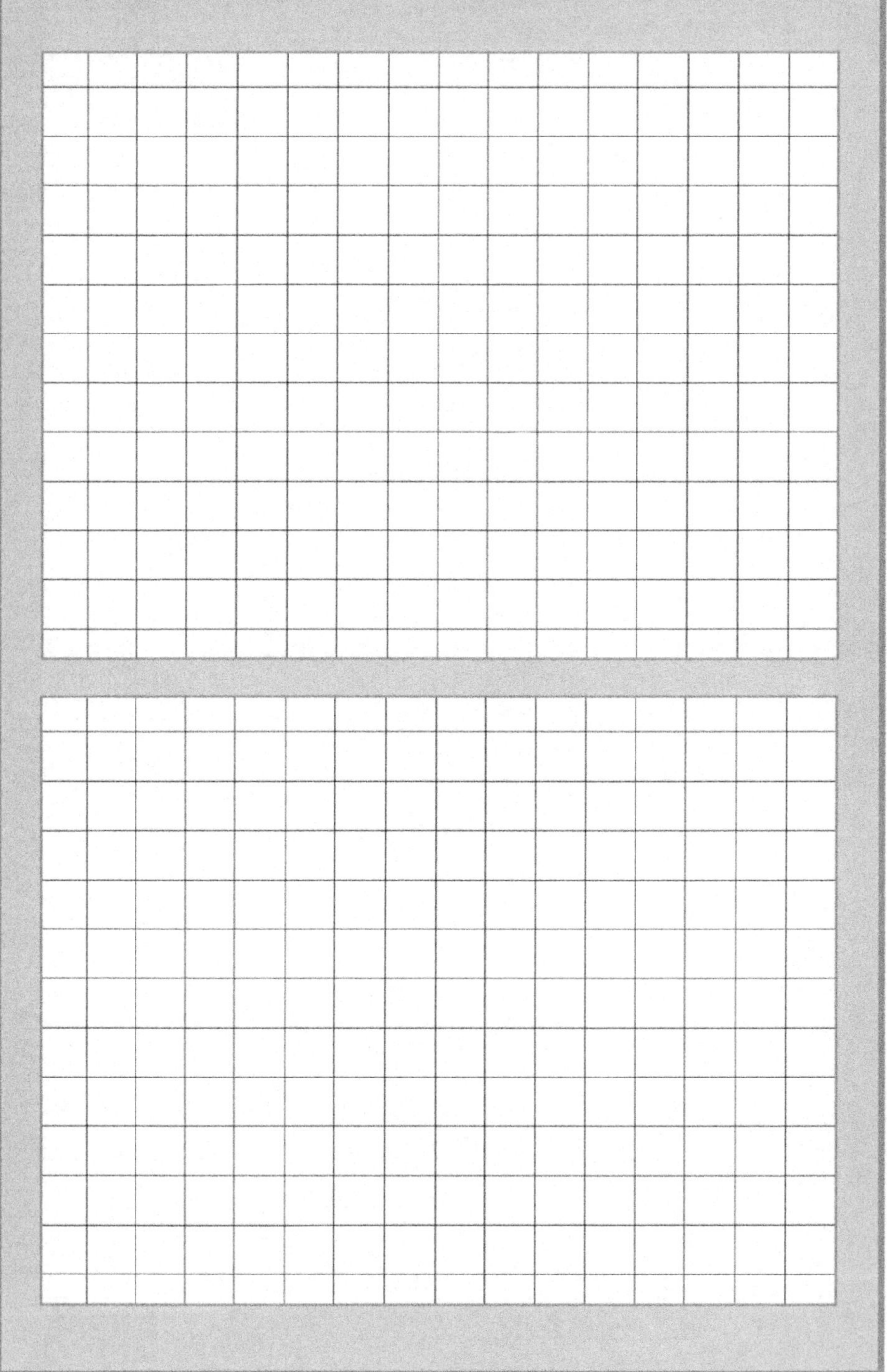

HOME RENOVATION / ROOM PLANNER

ROOM REQUIREMENTS

DECOR & STYLE

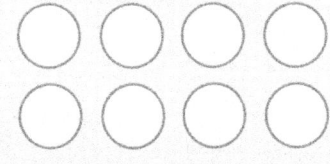

COLOURS

SKETCH PLANS

HOME RENOVATION / PROGRESS TRACKER

WEEKLY GOALS

QUESTIONS & ISSUES

TO-DO'S

MATERIALS LIST

HOME RENOVATION / ROOM PLANNING GRIDS

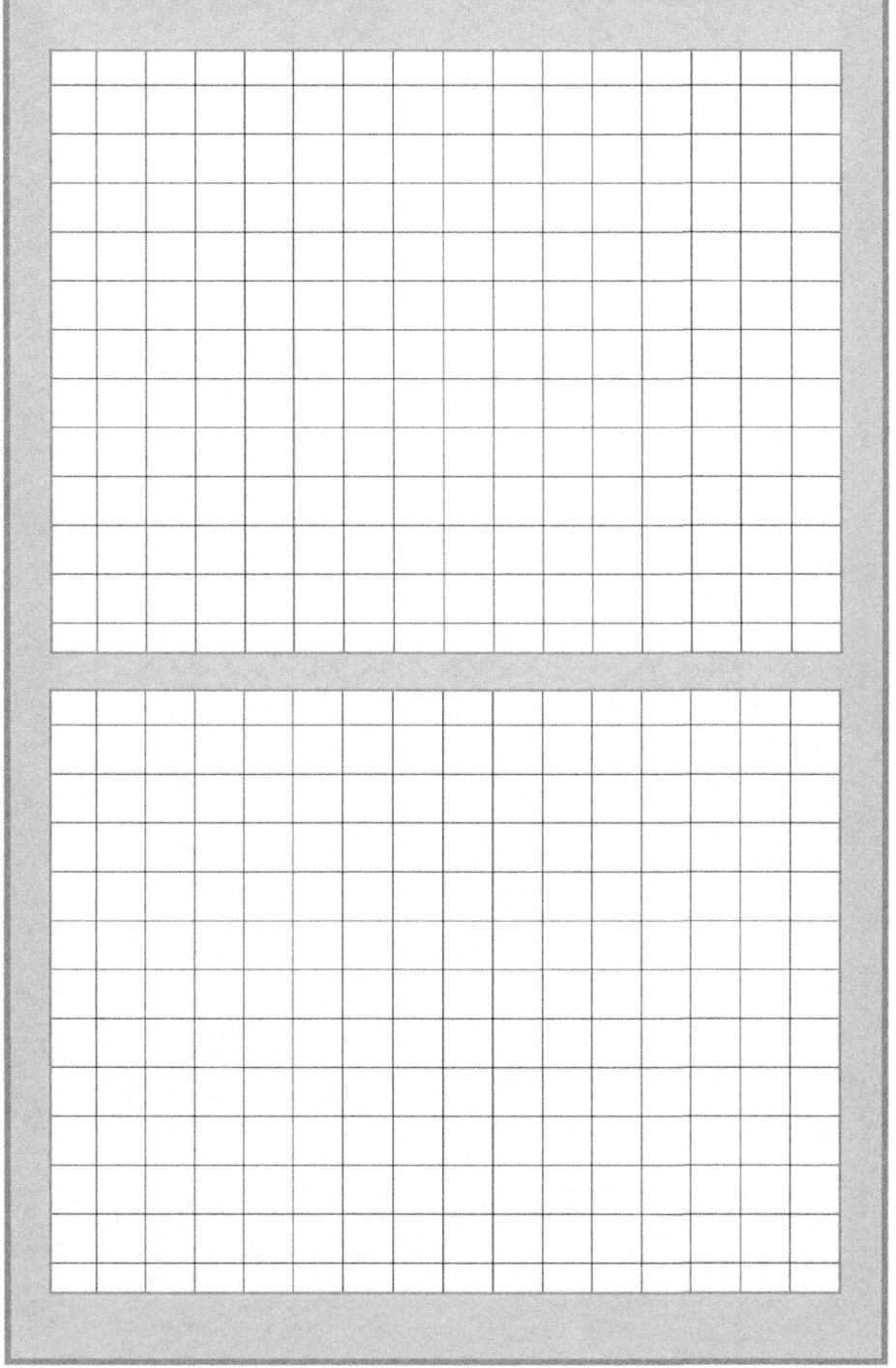

HOME RENOVATION / ROOM PLANNER

ROOM REQUIREMENTS

DECOR & STYLE

COLOURS

SKETCH PLANS

HOME RENOVATION / PROGRESS TRACKER

WEEKLY GOALS

QUESTIONS & ISSUES

TO-DO'S

MATERIALS LIST

HOME RENOVATION / ROOM PLANNING GRIDS

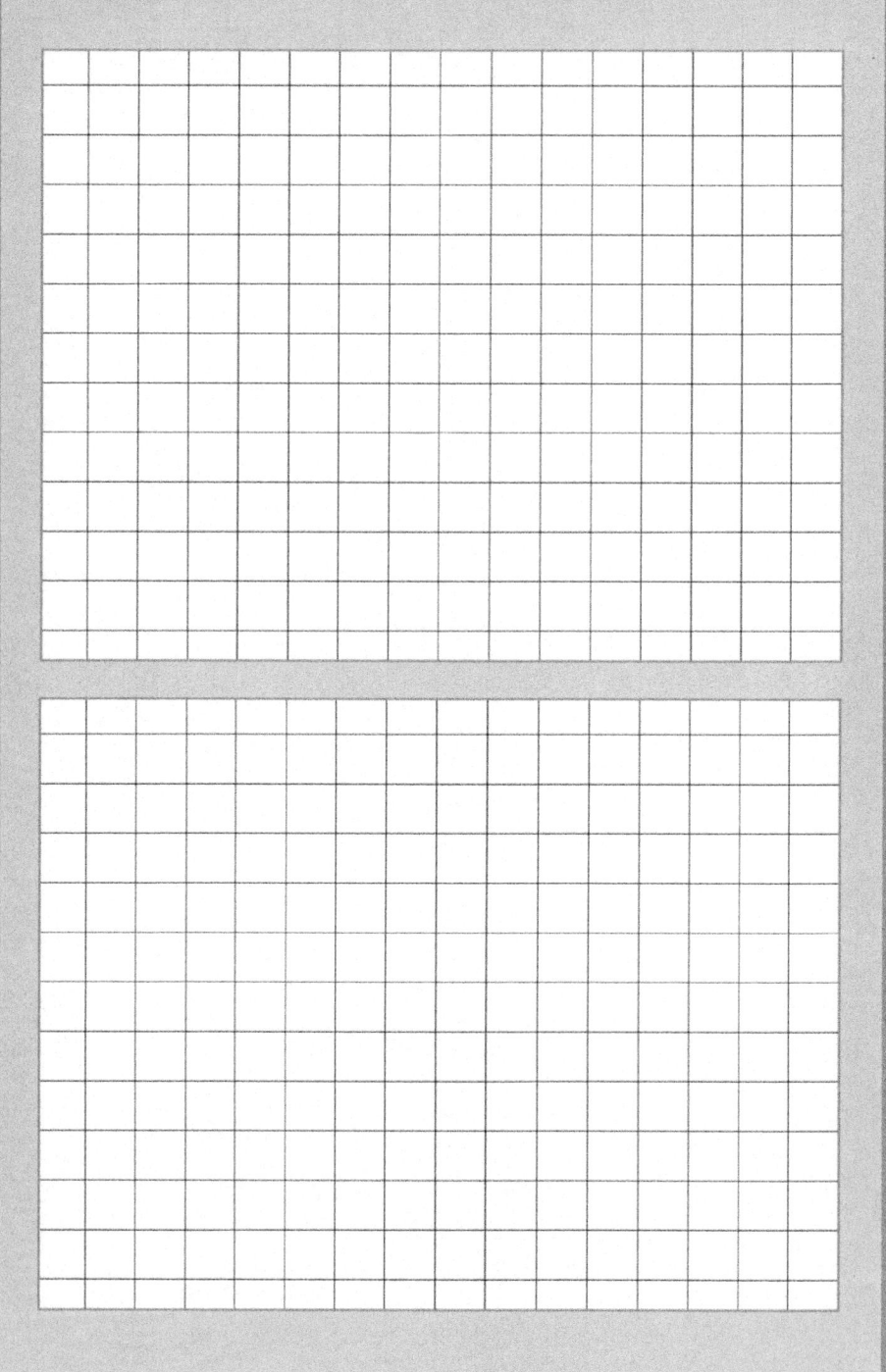

HOME RENOVATION / ROOM PLANNER

ROOM REQUIREMENTS

DECOR & STYLE

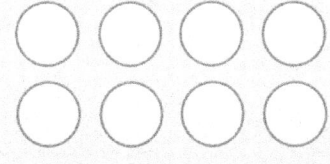

COLOURS

SKETCH PLANS

HOME RENOVATION / PROGRESS TRACKER

WEEKLY GOALS

QUESTIONS & ISSUES

TO-DO'S

MATERIALS LIST

HOME RENOVATION / ROOM PLANNING GRIDS

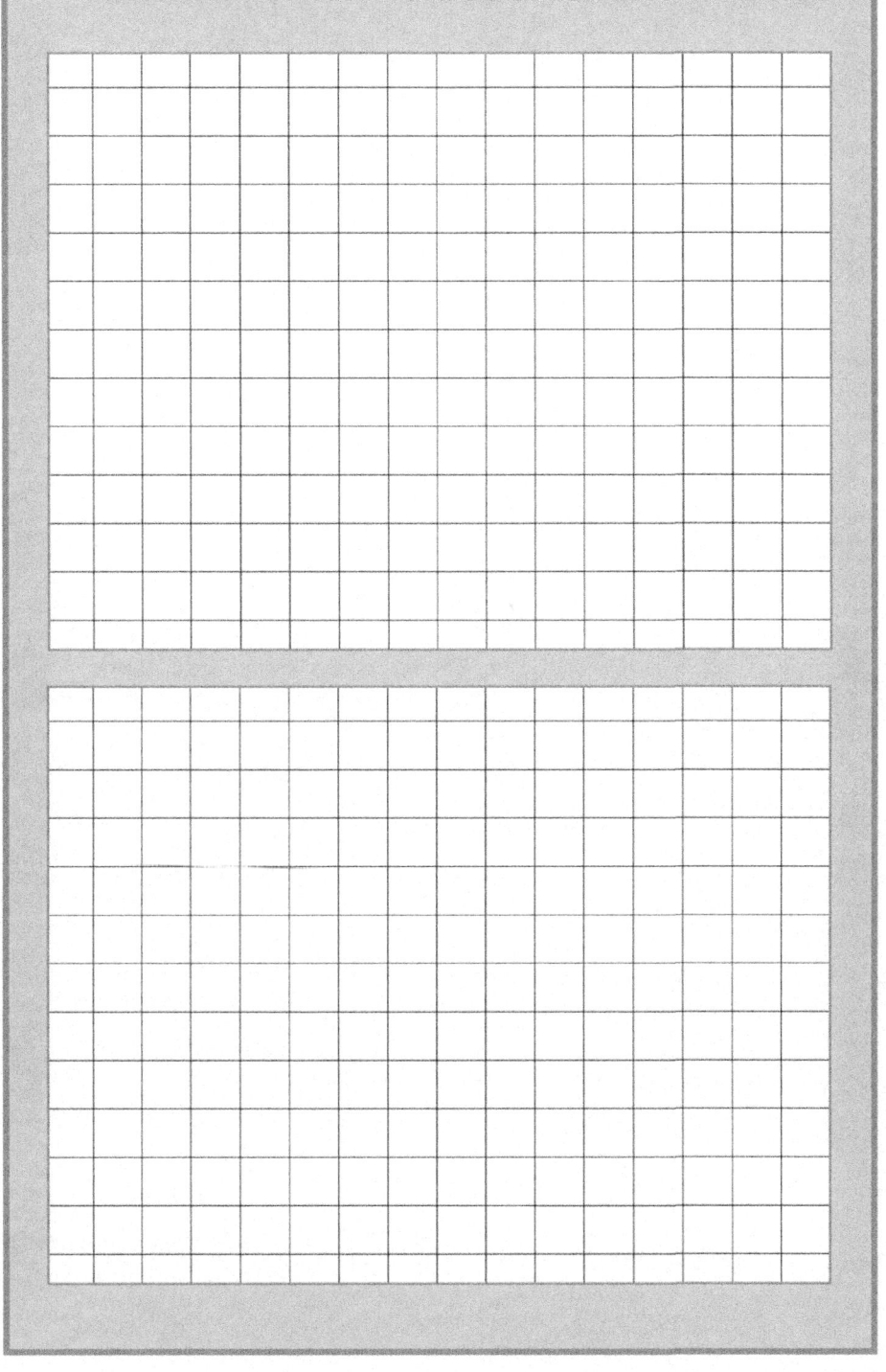

HOME RENOVATION / ROOM PLANNER

ROOM REQUIREMENTS

DECOR & STYLE

COLOURS

SKETCH PLANS

HOME RENOVATION / PROGRESS TRACKER

WEEKLY GOALS

QUESTIONS & ISSUES

TO-DO'S

MATERIALS LIST

HOME RENOVATION / ROOM PLANNING GRIDS

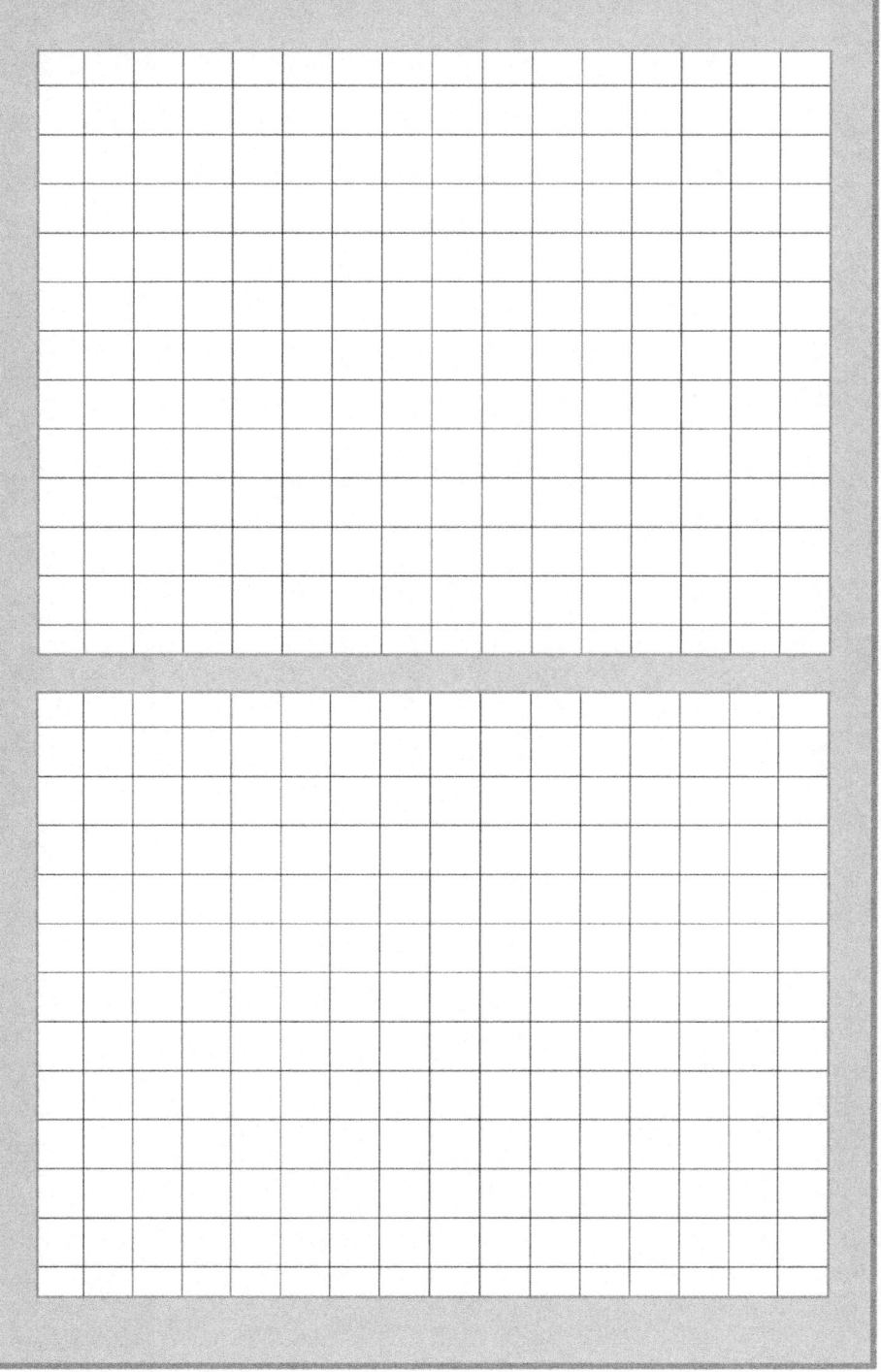

HOME RENOVATION / ROOM PLANNER

ROOM REQUIREMENTS

DECOR & STYLE

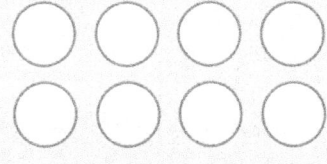

COLOURS

SKETCH PLANS

HOME RENOVATION / PROGRESS TRACKER

WEEKLY GOALS

QUESTIONS & ISSUES

TO-DO'S

MATERIALS LIST

HOME RENOVATION / ROOM PLANNING GRIDS

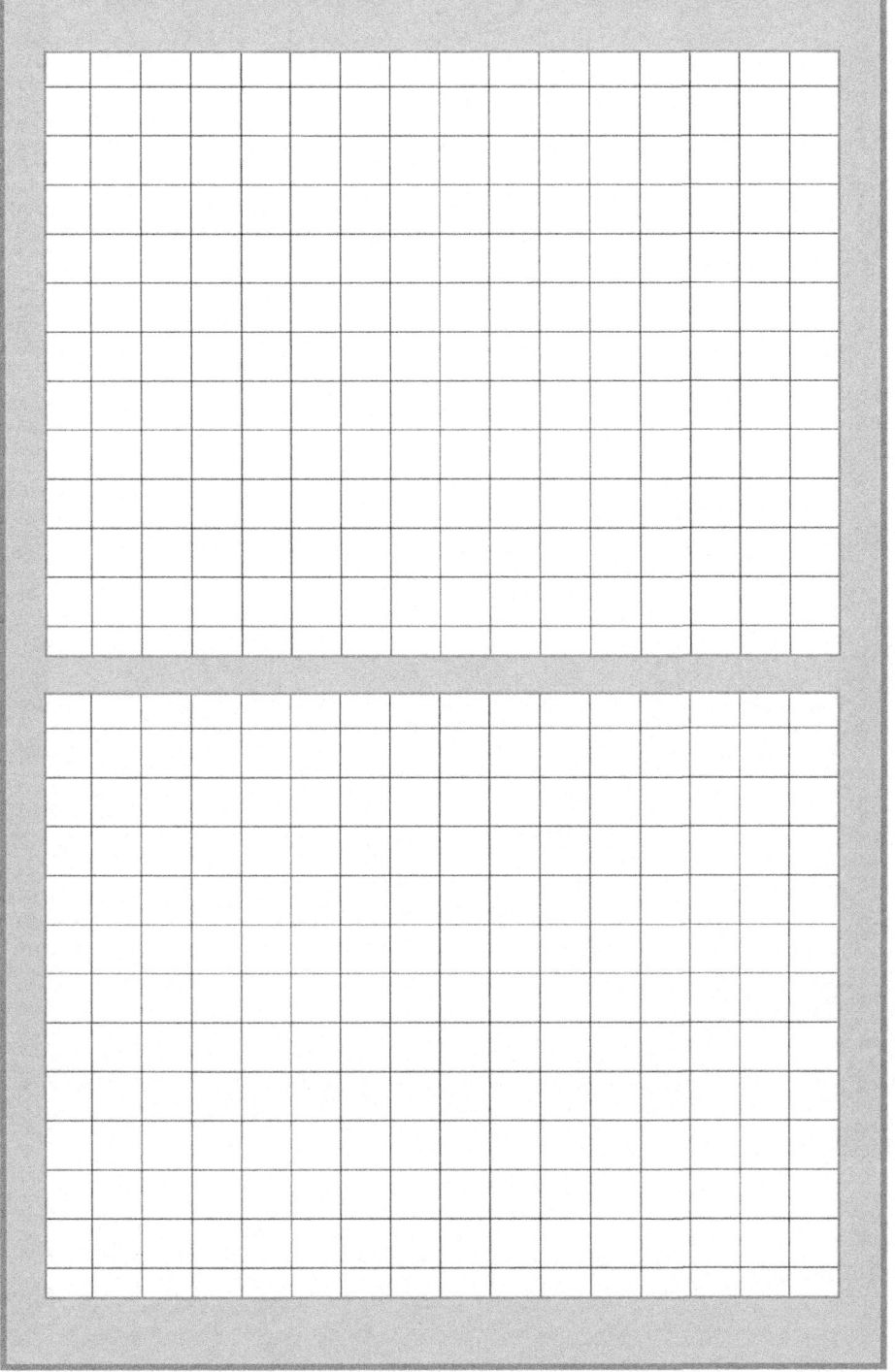

HOME RENOVATION / ROOM PLANNER

ROOM REQUIREMENTS

DECOR & STYLE

COLOURS

SKETCH PLANS

HOME RENOVATION / PROGRESS TRACKER

WEEKLY GOALS

QUESTIONS & ISSUES

TO-DO'S

MATERIALS LIST

HOME RENOVATION / ROOM PLANNING GRIDS

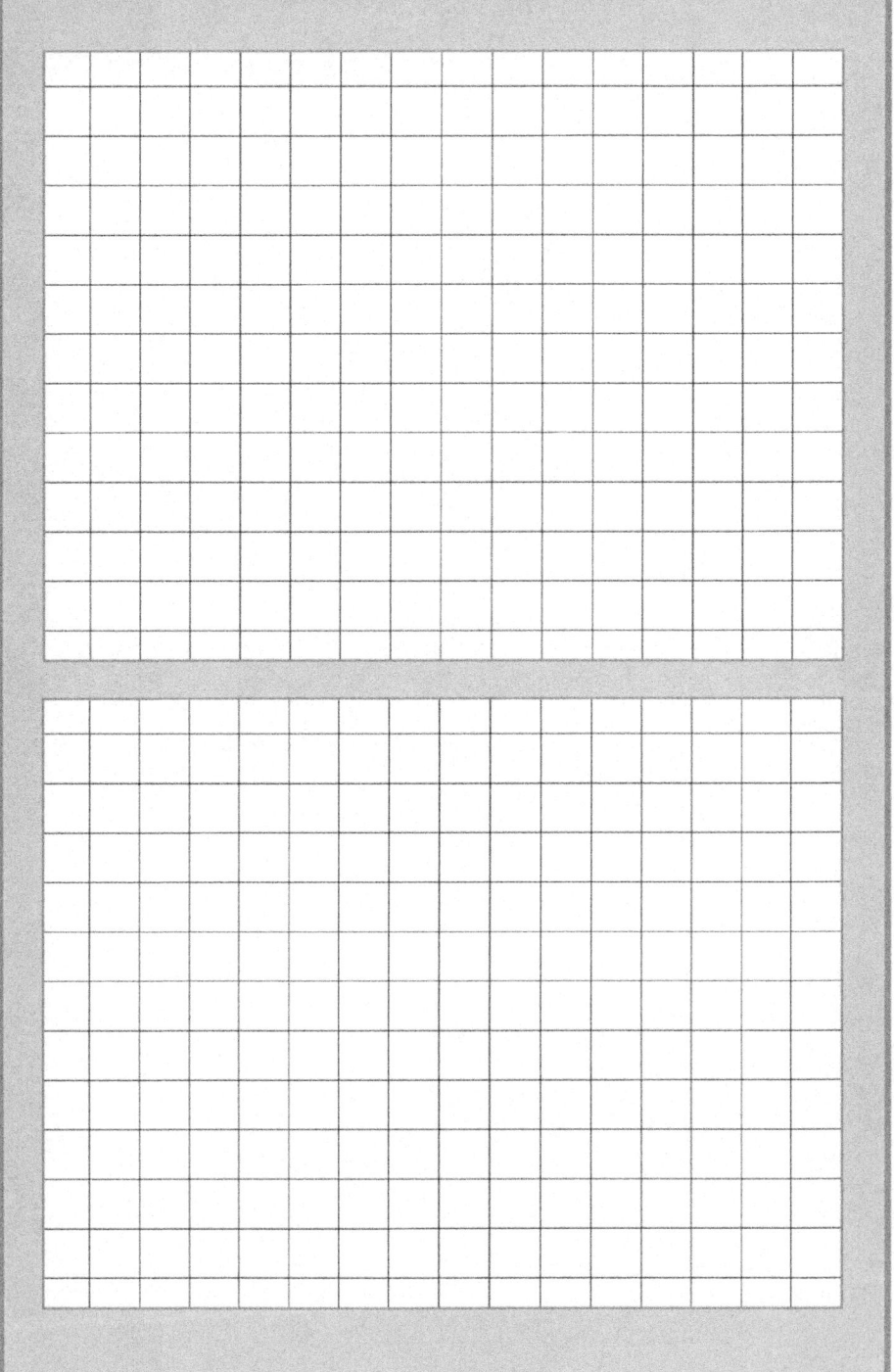

HOME RENOVATION / ROOM PLANNER

ROOM REQUIREMENTS

DECOR & STYLE

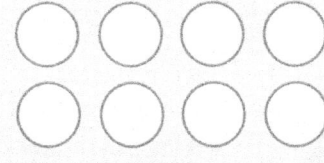

COLOURS

SKETCH PLANS

HOME RENOVATION / PROGRESS TRACKER

WEEKLY GOALS

QUESTIONS & ISSUES

TO-DO'S

MATERIALS LIST

HOME RENOVATION / ROOM PLANNING GRIDS

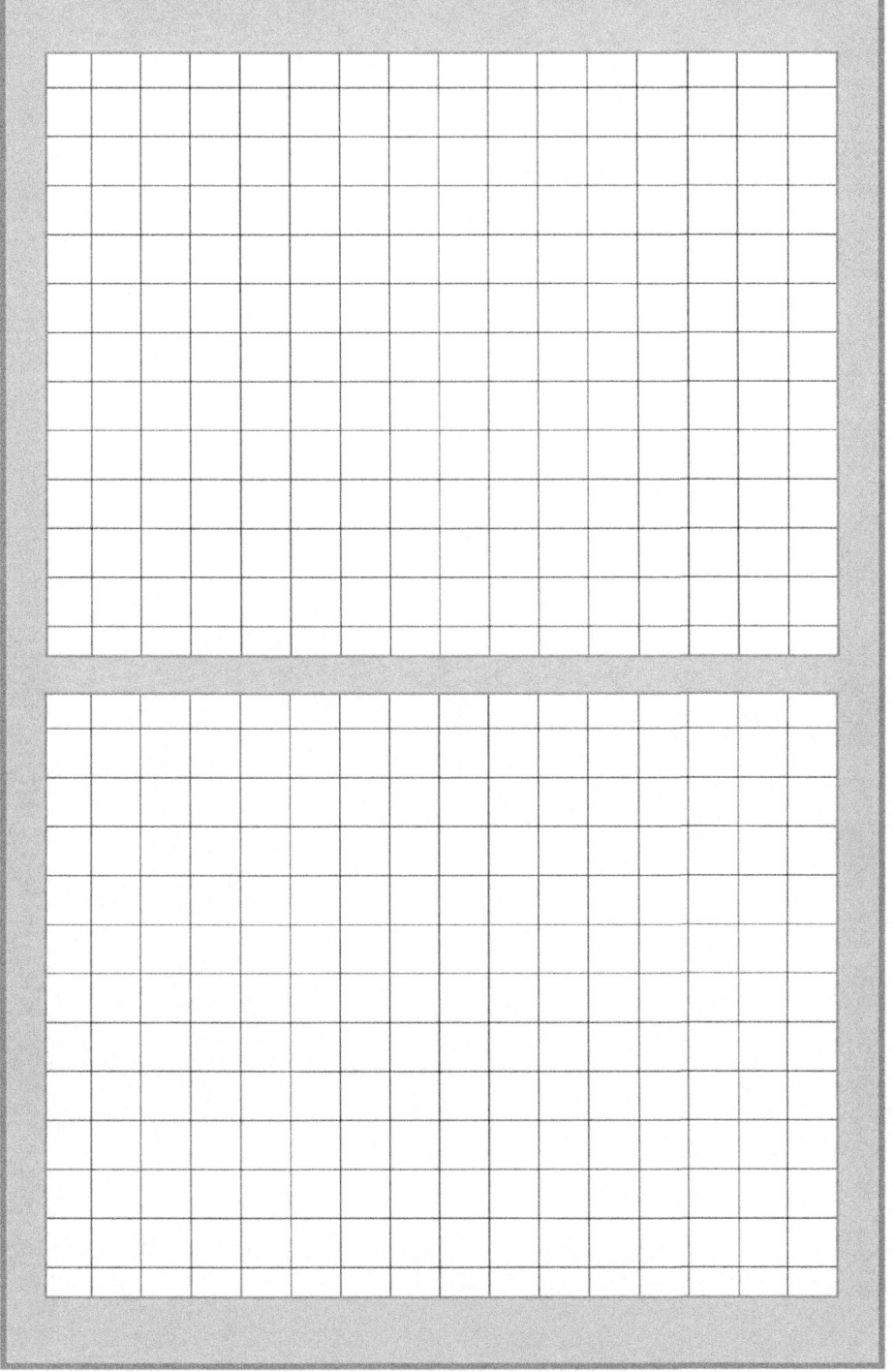

HOME RENOVATION / ROOM PLANNER

ROOM REQUIREMENTS

DECOR & STYLE

COLOURS

SKETCH PLANS

HOME RENOVATION / PROGRESS TRACKER

WEEKLY GOALS

QUESTIONS & ISSUES

TO-DO'S

MATERIALS LIST

HOME RENOVATION / ROOM PLANNING GRIDS

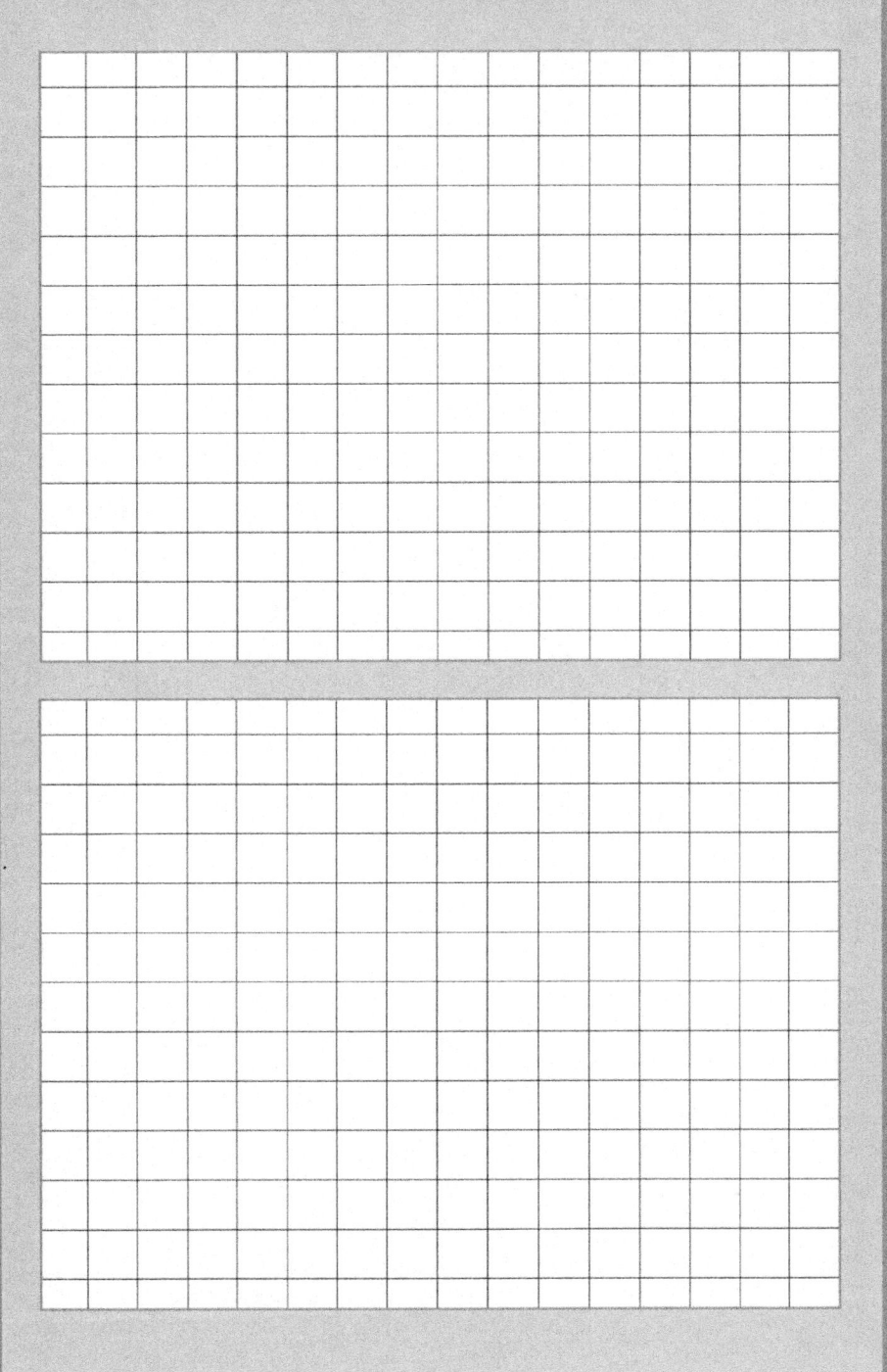

HOME RENOVATION / ROOM PLANNER

ROOM REQUIREMENTS

DECOR & STYLE

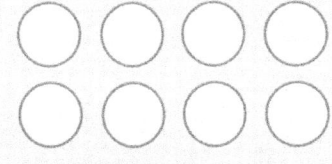

COLOURS

SKETCH PLANS

HOME RENOVATION / PROGRESS TRACKER

WEEKLY GOALS

QUESTIONS & ISSUES

TO-DO'S

MATERIALS LIST

HOME RENOVATION / ROOM PLANNING GRIDS

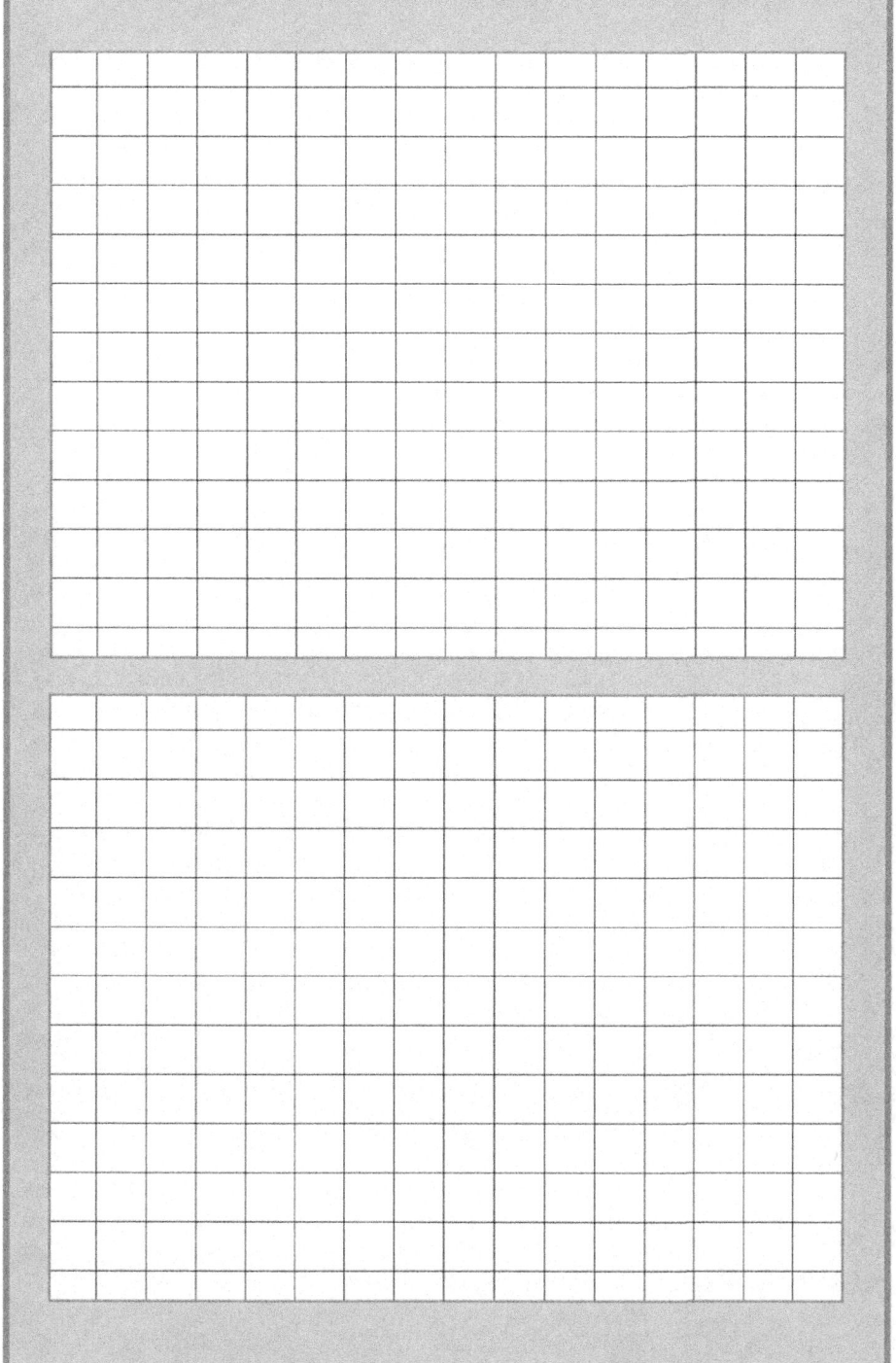

HOME RENOVATION / ROOM PLANNER

ROOM REQUIREMENTS

DECOR & STYLE

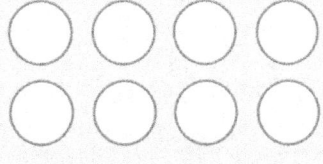

COLOURS

SKETCH PLANS

HOME RENOVATION / PROGRESS TRACKER

WEEKLY GOALS

QUESTIONS & ISSUES

TO-DO'S

MATERIALS LIST

HOME RENOVATION / ROOM PLANNING GRIDS

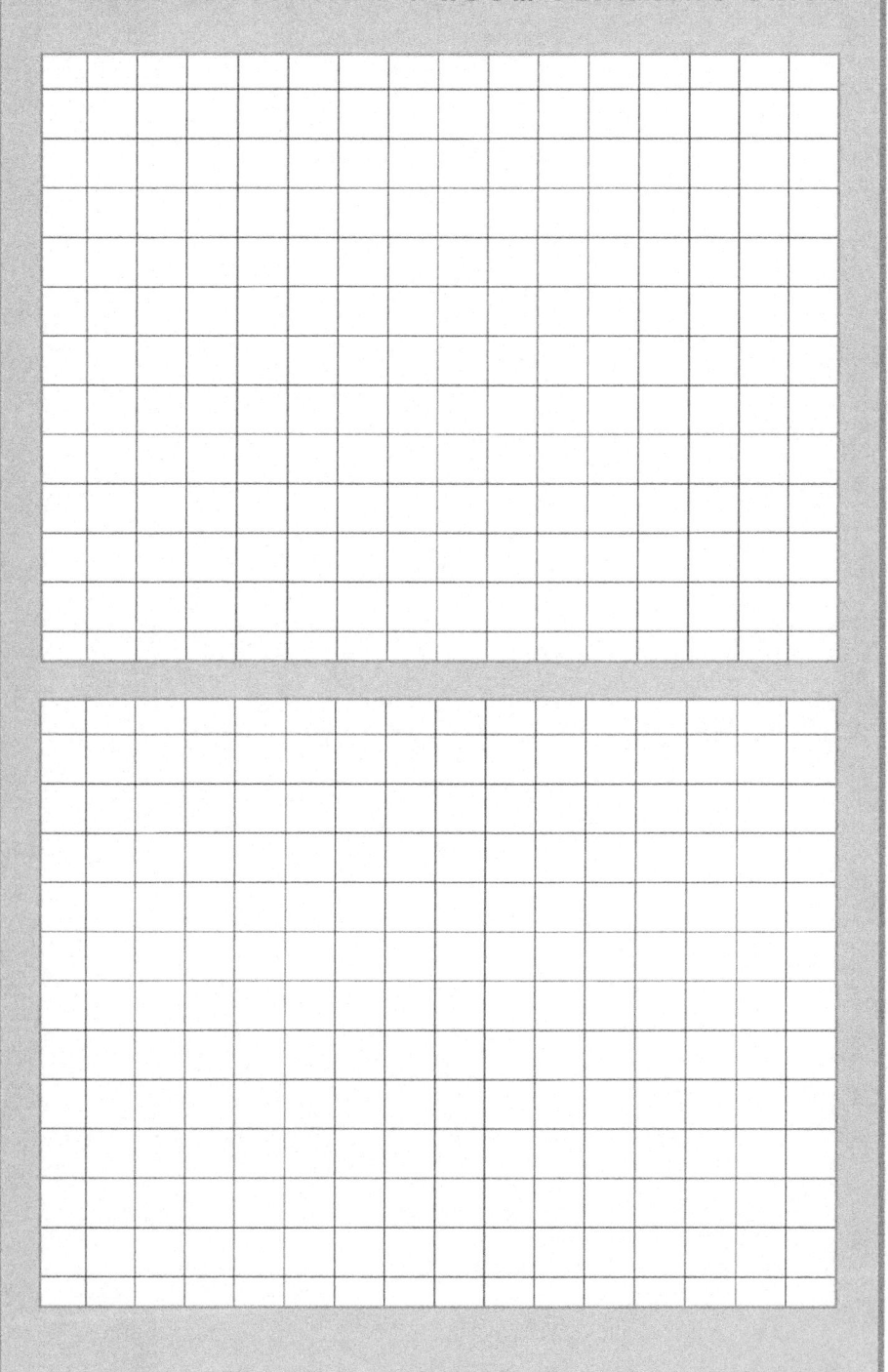

HOME RENOVATION / ROOM PLANNER

ROOM REQUIREMENTS

DECOR & STYLE

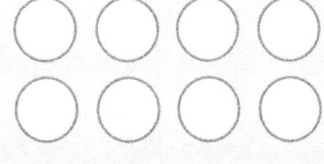

COLOURS

SKETCH PLANS

HOME RENOVATION / PROGRESS TRACKER

WEEKLY GOALS

QUESTIONS & ISSUES

TO-DO'S

MATERIALS LIST

HOME RENOVATION / ROOM PLANNING GRIDS

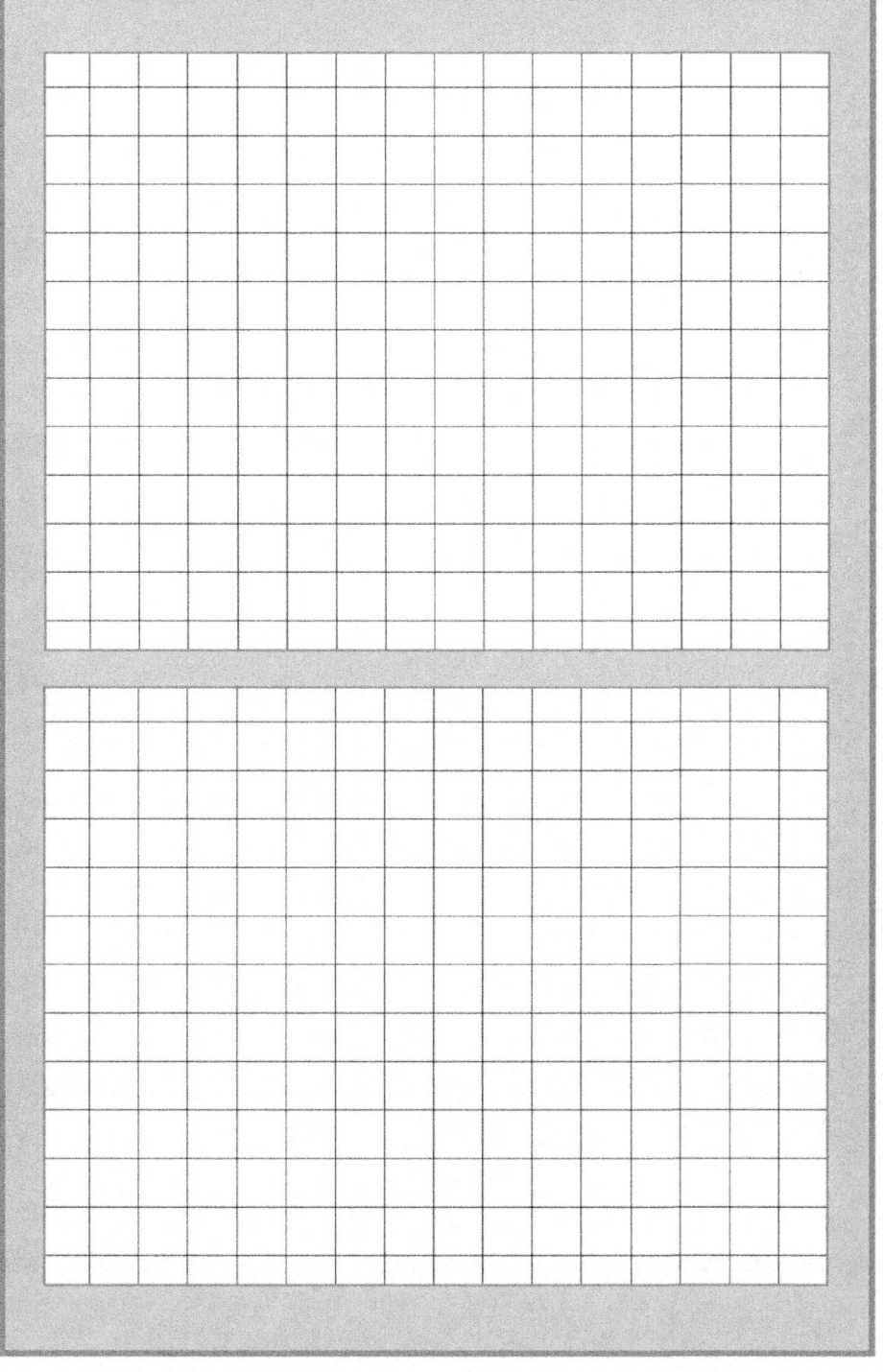

HOME RENOVATION / ROOM PLANNER

ROOM REQUIREMENTS

DECOR & STYLE

COLOURS

SKETCH PLANS

HOME RENOVATION / PROGRESS TRACKER

WEEKLY GOALS

QUESTIONS & ISSUES

TO-DO'S

MATERIALS LIST

HOME RENOVATION / ROOM PLANNING GRIDS

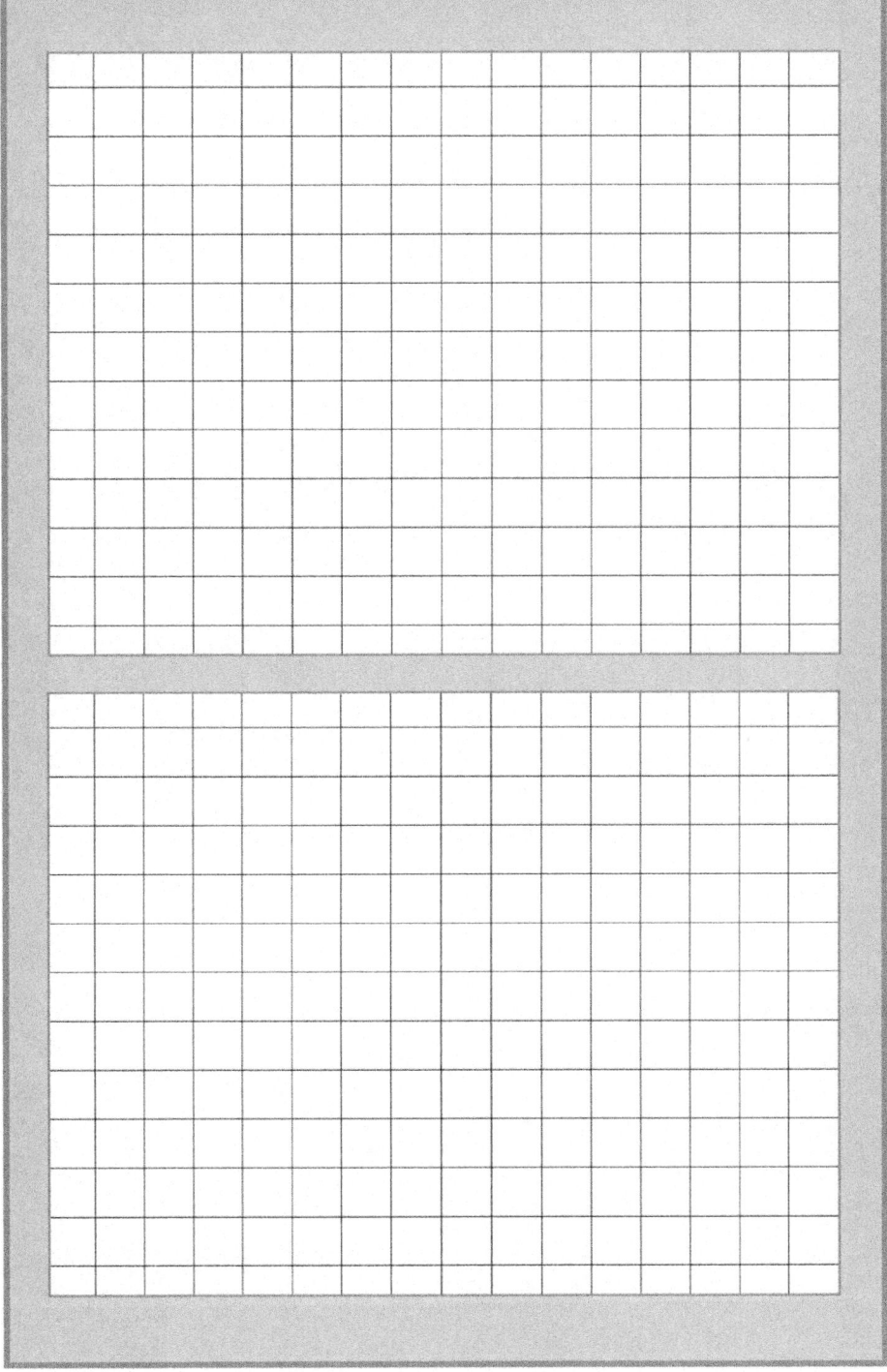

HOME RENOVATION / ROOM PLANNER

ROOM REQUIREMENTS

DECOR & STYLE

COLOURS

SKETCH PLANS

HOME RENOVATION / PROGRESS TRACKER

WEEKLY GOALS

QUESTIONS & ISSUES

TO-DO'S

MATERIALS LIST

HOME RENOVATION / ROOM PLANNING GRIDS

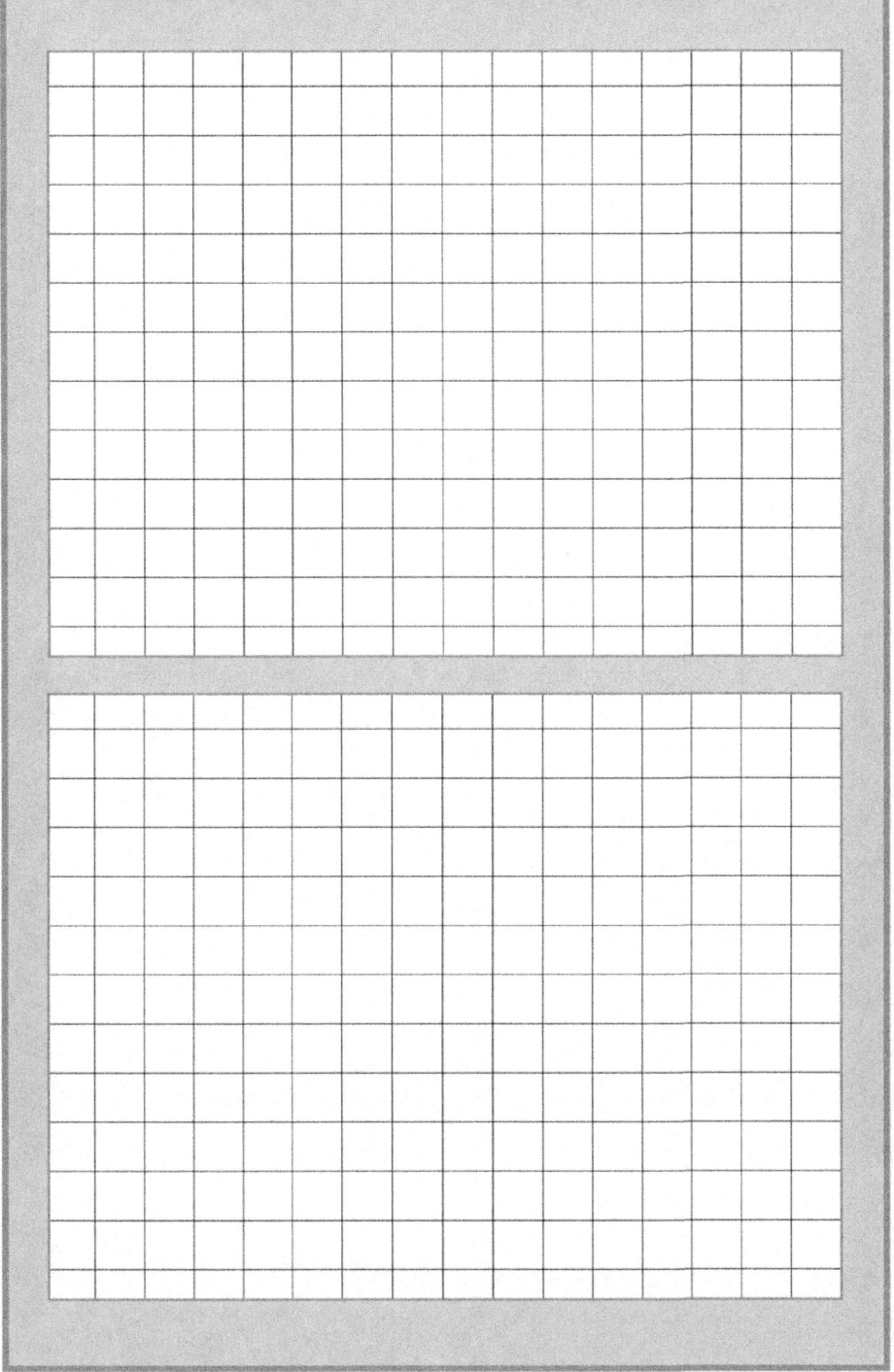

HOME RENOVATION / ROOM PLANNER

ROOM REQUIREMENTS

DECOR & STYLE

COLOURS

SKETCH PLANS

HOME RENOVATION / PROGRESS TRACKER

WEEKLY GOALS

QUESTIONS & ISSUES

TO-DO'S

MATERIALS LIST

HOME RENOVATION / ROOM PLANNING GRIDS

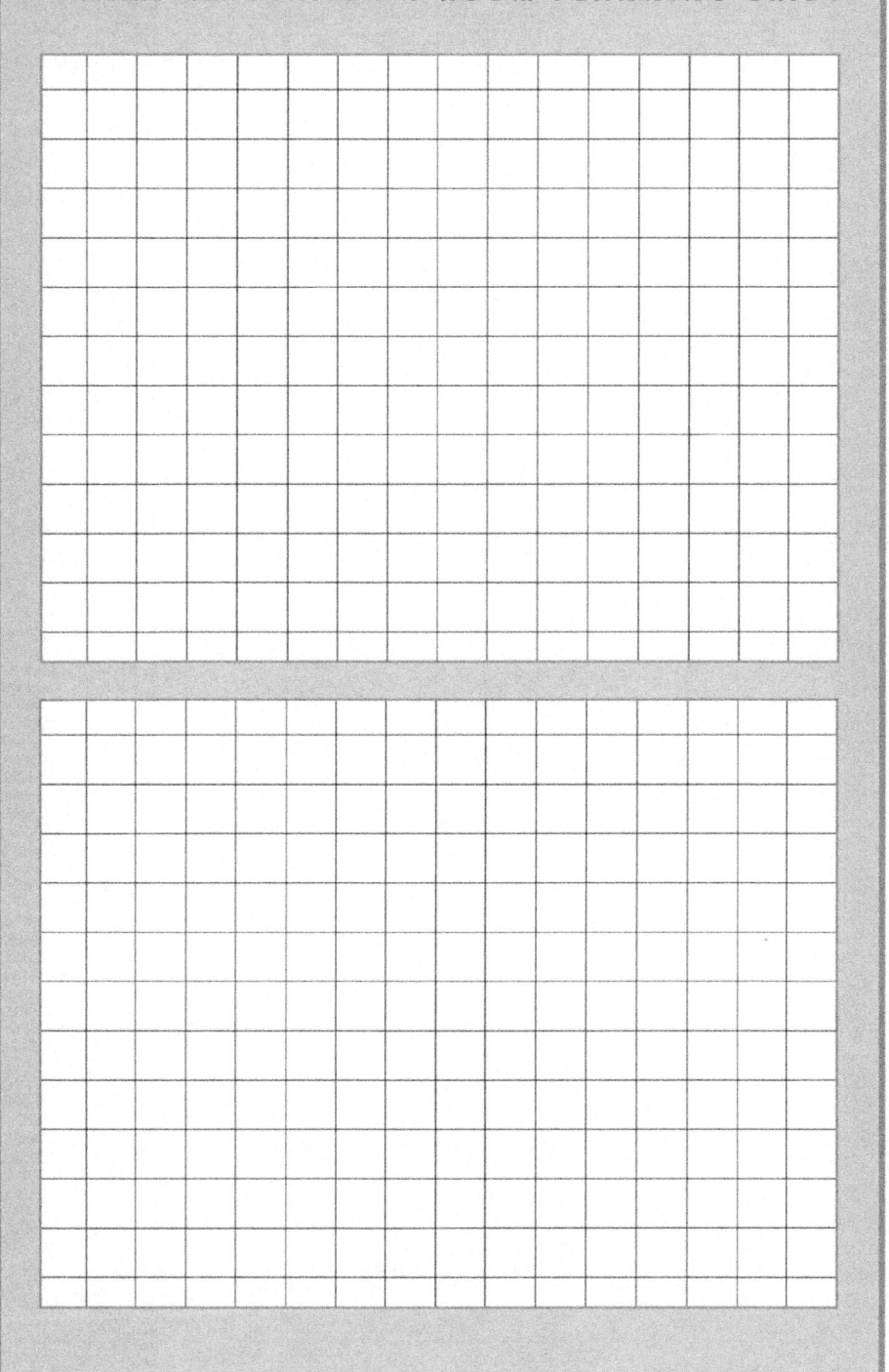

HOME RENOVATION / ROOM PLANNER

ROOM REQUIREMENTS

DECOR & STYLE

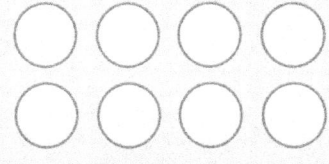

COLOURS

SKETCH PLANS

HOME RENOVATION / PROGRESS TRACKER

WEEKLY GOALS

QUESTIONS & ISSUES

TO-DO'S

MATERIALS LIST

HOME RENOVATION / ROOM PLANNING GRIDS

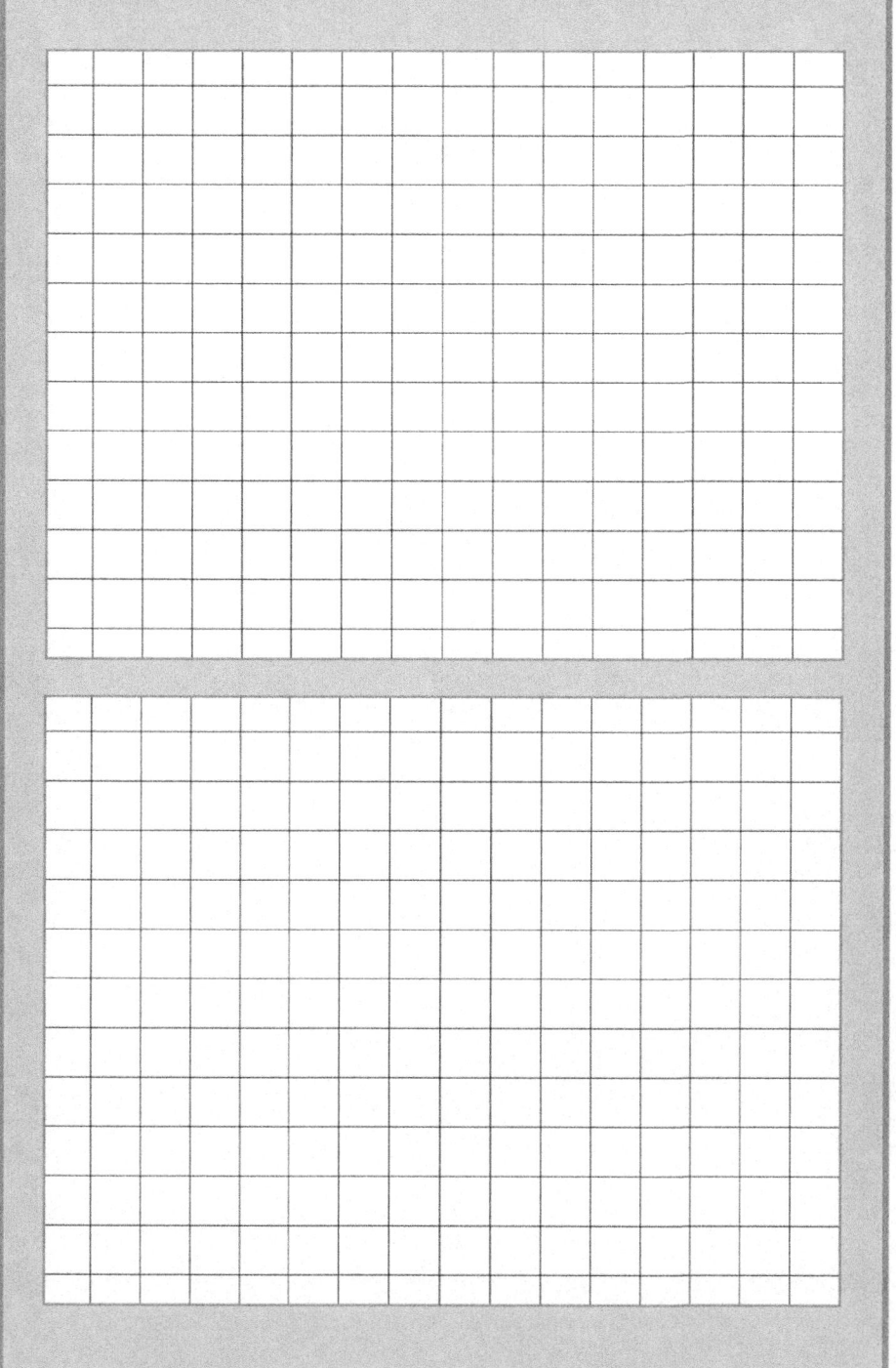

HOME RENOVATION / ROOM PLANNER

ROOM REQUIREMENTS

DECOR & STYLE

COLOURS

SKETCH PLANS

HOME RENOVATION / PROGRESS TRACKER

WEEKLY GOALS

QUESTIONS & ISSUES

TO-DO'S

MATERIALS LIST

HOME RENOVATION / ROOM PLANNING GRIDS

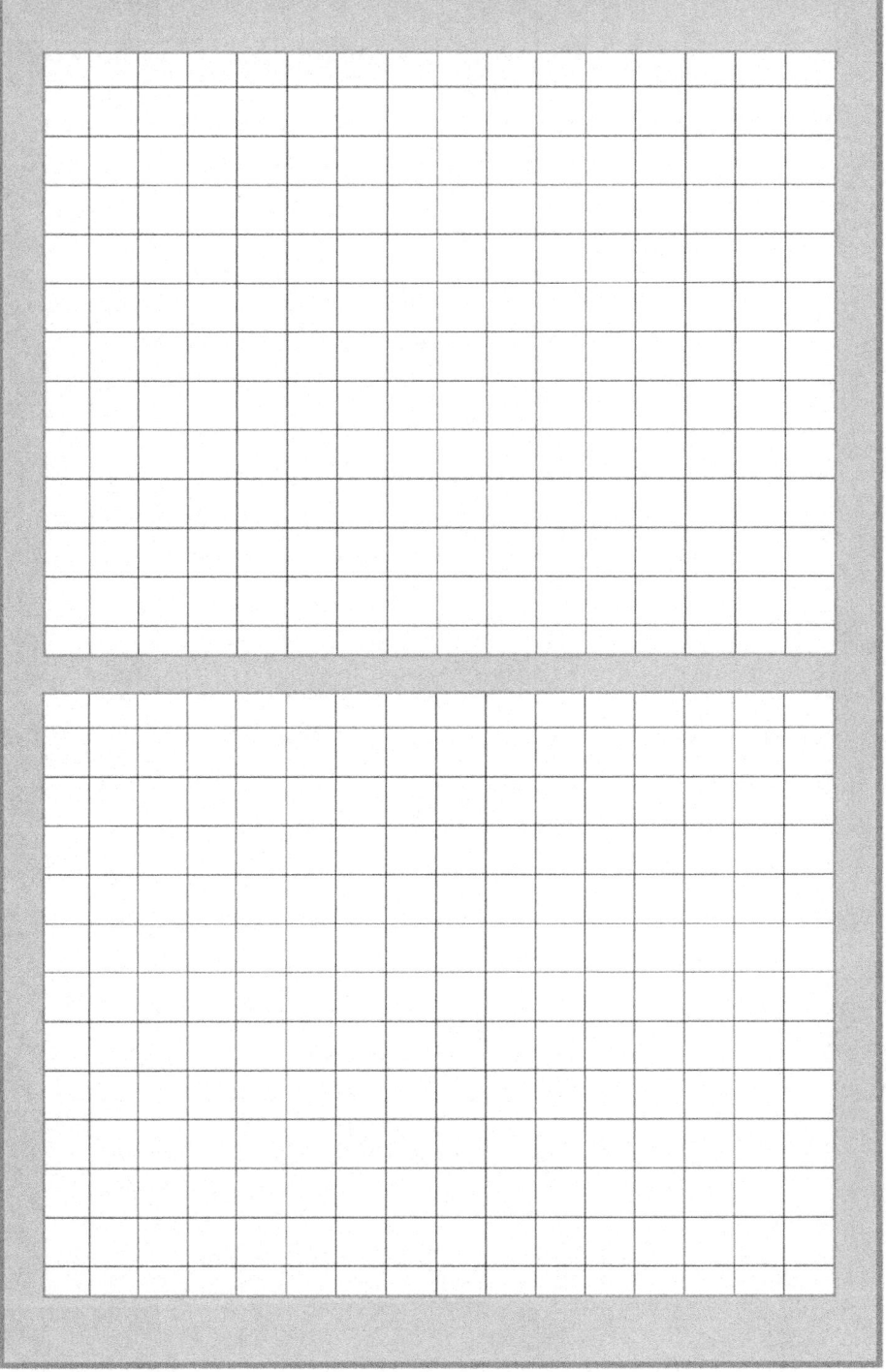

HOME RENOVATION / ROOM PLANNER

ROOM REQUIREMENTS

DECOR & STYLE

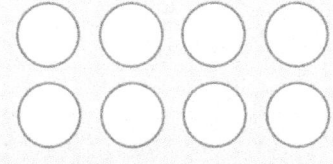

COLOURS

SKETCH PLANS

HOME RENOVATION / PROGRESS TRACKER

WEEKLY GOALS

QUESTIONS & ISSUES

TO-DO'S

MATERIALS LIST

HOME RENOVATION / ROOM PLANNING GRIDS

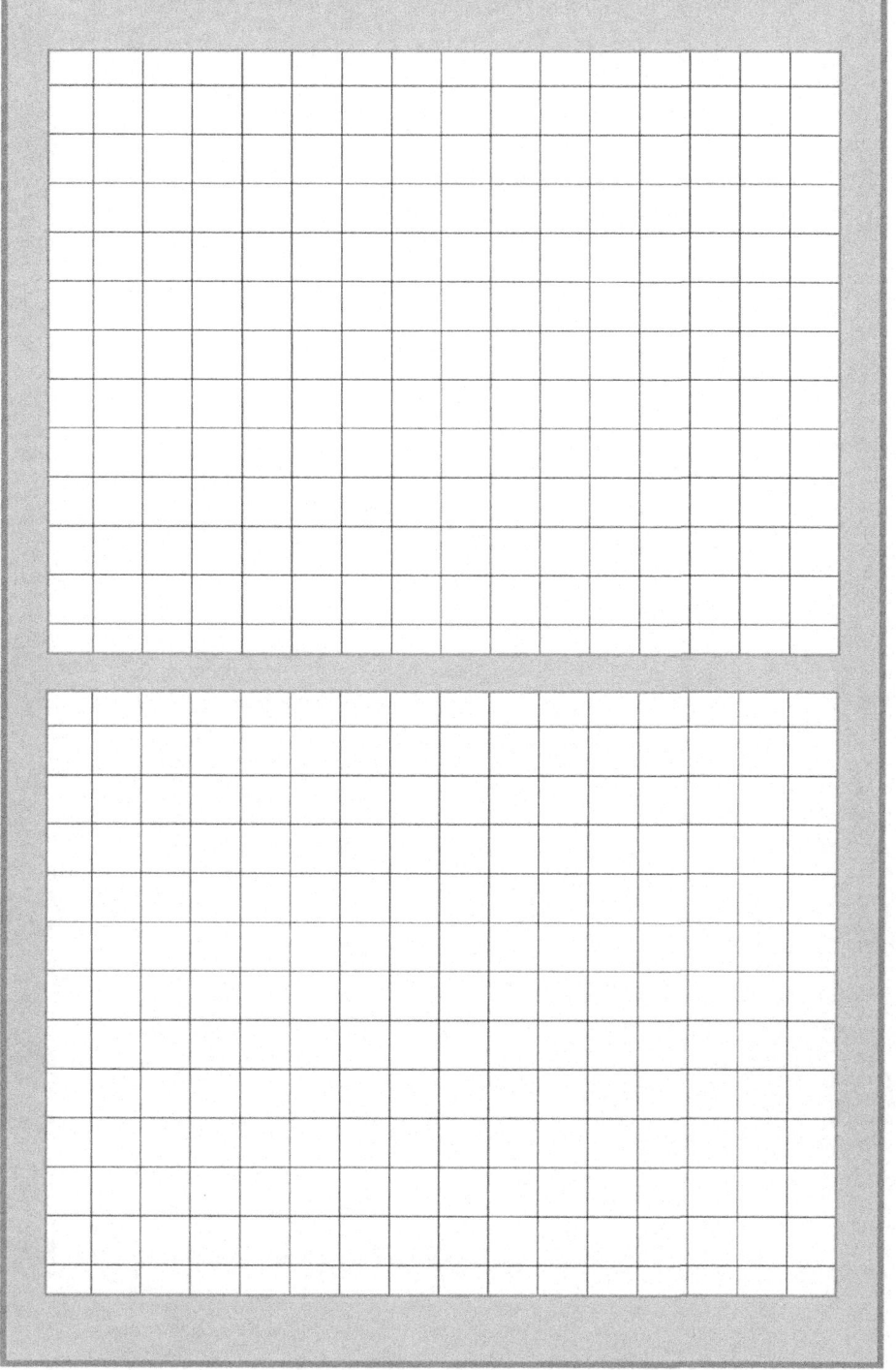

HOME RENOVATION / ROOM PLANNER

ROOM REQUIREMENTS

DECOR & STYLE

COLOURS

SKETCH PLANS

HOME RENOVATION / PROGRESS TRACKER

WEEKLY GOALS

QUESTIONS & ISSUES

TO-DO'S

MATERIALS LIST

HOME RENOVATION / ROOM PLANNING GRIDS

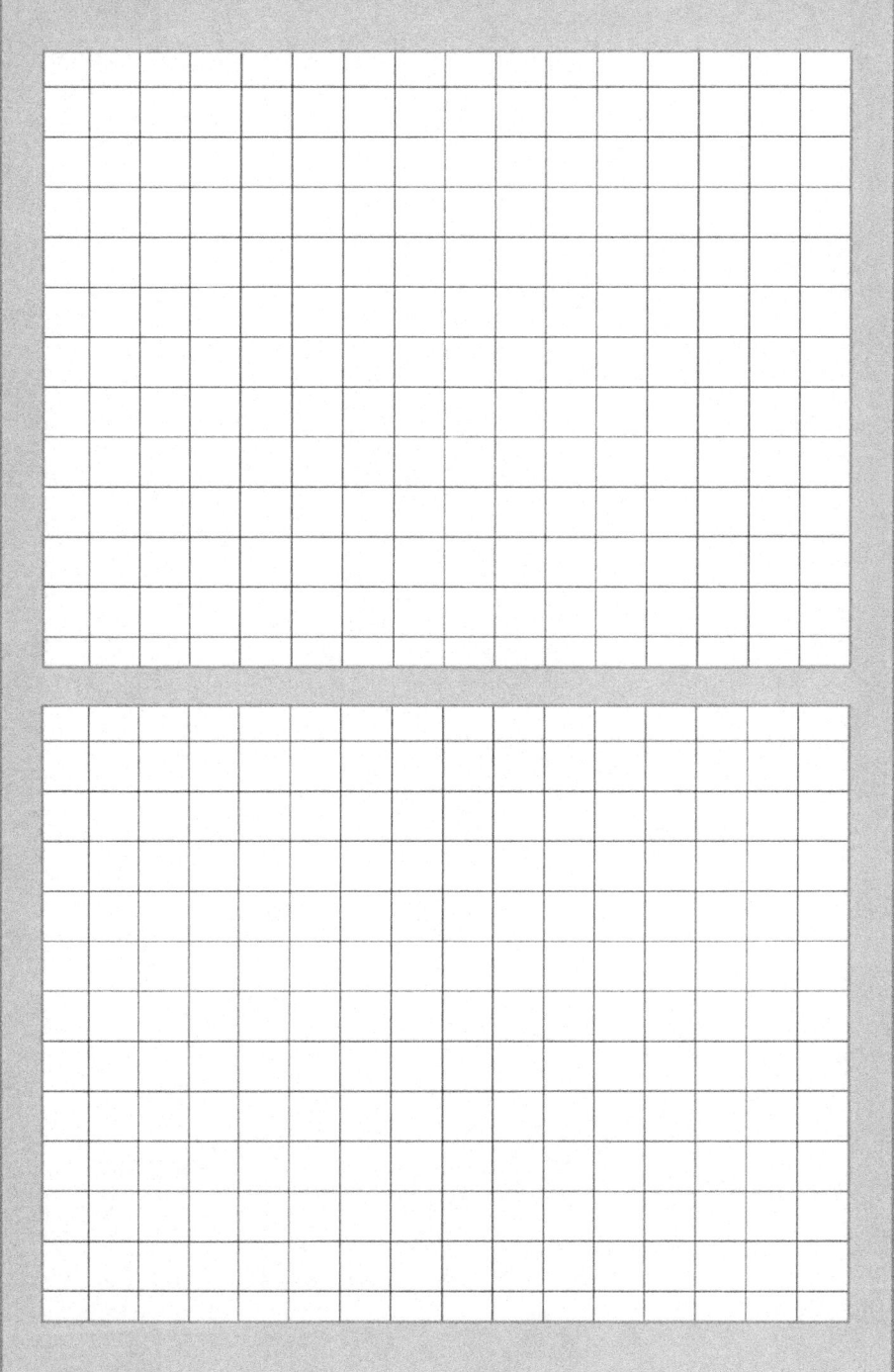

Printed in Great Britain
by Amazon